Mitchell Woodiwiss Publishing

Printed in the U.S.A.
www.CamillesCooking.com

ISBN-10   0989471500
ISBN-13   978-0-989471503

Foodships

Living Life…One Recipe at a Time

By

Camille Orrichio Loccisano

To the dear Roggeman Family,

Thank you for the blessing of Tom ("Rock")!!

Love,
Camille

3

Dedicated to my children,

Francesco, Nicholas and Christopher

Table of Contents

Introduction

Think of a mouthwatering recipe that reminds you of a special person or an eventful time in your life. That is foodships! Behind many recipes there are stories and memories of the nurturing relationships that enrich our lives, and that is what this cookbook is all about. Foodships is the meaningful connection of food and relationships. It is a reminder that life is one long, feasting journey weaving events and people with the taste of memorable flavors.

As adults, we fondly remember childhood food experiences. Certain gratifying aromas transport us back in time to the people and places we care about and love. We recall family and friends gathered around festive tables filled with platters and bowls that captured brilliant flavors and an edible passion that connects us all. In the spirit of comfort, we often duplicate those tastes that are such a pleasant reminder of days gone by, and through all the years of our lives, food continues to bring us together, as it has such a presence among our relations with others. Often through these shared experiences, further bonds are developed, more memories are made, and relationships thrive. Thus, we have foodships! Very simply, food is the great communicator, and this is true whether we are the cook, the one who admires and eats the cooking, or both.

Since this cookbook is about life, that means it is a real pilgrimage that is not limited to sweet happenings and rose-colored glasses. As well as the good days of kindness and pleasant passion, life is also host to days of raw struggle. Food is also present during such times, and it is often a small tool for inspiration, healing and emerging even stronger than before the unfortunate period of time occurred.

My oldest son, Frankie, passed away at the age of seventeen. In his wake, I am left to live the remaining days of my life as a healing process. Suffice it to say, you never recover emotionally from the loss of a child, but you try, for the sake of those you love, to move forward. This has caused me to be on an everlasting trek to find ways to simply feel better each day.

In the weeks following Frankie's passing, I was not sure if I would ever be able to do some of the ordinary tasks of life or even the most pleasurable of activities that I once enjoyed. For me, cooking and food have always been a combination of the two, and it is also my profession. As a single mom of three sons, of course cooking is one of my tasks. But happily, for me, I have always been a complete and dedicated "food romantic," a person who loves to cook and taste, respects the entire culinary world, and cherishes her kitchen, both professionally and personally. Food and cooking have been one of the greatest joys of my life. It is that simple.

Now back to those weeks after Frankie's passing. I realized that eventually I would have to cook again. I truly did not know how I was going to step back into my kitchen, among my many cooking tools and my ingredients and recipes, when I knew that Frankie would not be with me to claim the tasting moment. Never again would I hear his approval of a new dish I created, or his advice on how I should add a dash of this or a pinch of that.

Yet, I marched into my kitchen and purposely cooked Frankie's favorite meal. I was not sure how I would handle such an activity. But, as I continued, a certain sense of peace came to my fractured soul. I was able to do something that I always did for Frankie, and I was still able to cook something that he enjoyed eating. Frankie, in a sense, was still here! I could serve this meal to friends and family and recall happy conversations and times with my son when we had enjoyed these flavors in the past. I could even serve it to new friends who might have never known my son. I could tell them that this was my son's favorite meal, this dish was part of my son's life, and they were now sharing in a small part of who he was and what he enjoyed. This is, without a doubt, my ultimate foodship.

In part one of this book, "Tales," I will share with you lighthearted anecdotes, along with recipes, of how the combination of family, friends, and food can capture us for life in an unfailingly pure fashion.

In part two, "Treasures," you will meet special individuals and their recipes or a recipe they have inspired. I share how their vibrant energy touches the lives of others and leads us to an open door of inviting flavors.

And finally, part three, "Taste," allows me the opportunity to share some of the recipes in my own repertoire. I offer tips and skills that I accumulated from my years as a restaurant owner and caterer. My final recipe of this book will be the one I write of above, Frankie's favorite.

This is what food is able to do. It helps us to celebrate the best and offers a balm for the worst. It connects people who might have never known of each other, and more than anything, it carries on important legacies of those we love. ~ C.L.

Part One
Tales

You should look for someone to eat and drink with
before looking for something to eat and drink..." ~Epicurus

As we live the days of our lives, year after year, certain happenings stand out in our hearts and minds. Some are very happy, some just eventful, but yet so very memorable. The following tales lead us to how the seasons and the years roll along with the tide of family, friendship, and food.

Grandma Sue's Dessert

While most cookbooks end with the desserts, I opt to be unique at the beginning of this one. My very first story and recipe will be a dessert, and may I add, a very tantalizing one.

It all begins with Grandma Sue, who was not related by blood, but she was like a grandparent to me in every sense of the word. When I was growing up, she lived on the ground-floor apartment of my parents' Brooklyn home, and she was the perfect picture of an old-fashioned Italian grandmother. By the time I knew her, she was a widow in her senior years, with many gourmet recipes, mostly Italian, under her belt. I owe much of my lifelong romance with food to Grandma Sue, a warm and generous woman who had amazing cooking chops.

But before Grandma Sue became a loving grandmother, she lived a long, eventful life. She was born and raised in Italy, and came to the United States when she was a young woman. However, she did not arrive happily, for she left behind the great love of her life, a young man named Joseph. Sue's parents sent her to the United States to marry a widowed man, named Tom, who was the father of young children. Sue had no choice but to obey her strict Italian father, thus leaving behind the young man she loved dearly. She married Tom, and together, they had more children and raised a family.

Years later, when Sue was spending a day at Coney Island,

a popular beach community in Brooklyn, she saw Joseph, who now also lived in the United States. Although many years had passed, the heartbreak, for both of them, was still fresh and alive. They were both awestruck upon seeing each other after such a long period of time.

He asked her, "Why did you leave?"

She told him that she had no choice. Sue never saw Joseph again, except, of course, in her dreams, and never stopped loving him until the end of her days.

Sue experienced many more trials and tribulations along the course of life, including the loss of her teenage son to cancer. Yet, she was strong and spirited and also gave much joy to those around her, especially through her cooking. Her cozy apartment was always open to one and all in our Brooklyn neighborhood, and her kitchen was one of great activity. Always she was cooking and baking up crowd-pleasing meals and desserts. Her homemade pasta dishes were topped with savory sauces and sharp, flavorful cheeses. Her rich cakes would ooze with chocolate or luscious, sugary fruits.

As a child, I would sit at Grandma Sue's big wooden table while she instructed me on the fine art of cooking. While we chopped and cut, always she would tell me the stories of her life lessons while I learned to prepare the recipes in her outstanding repertoire. As I recall her words about her teenage son's passing, I realize the ironic and significant bridge that brought me from that table, as a careless and happy youth, to my present life, as a mother who also lost a teenage son to cancer, just like Grandma Sue.

Through it all, Grandma Sue continued to cook and bake. For me, the recipe that stands out most is a dessert that is really the most lush and indulgent dessert I have ever tasted. Yes, I know that is a strong statement, given how many wondrous and vast desserts are out there in the world.

Grandma Sue called this dessert *schkatalata*. Now, we knew this was an Italian dialect word, thus it was not the correct pronunciation, but nobody ever bothered to find out the proper way to pronounce the word. It was also not easy for us to gain further knowledge about this dessert because it was relatively unknown, at least in our Brooklyn community of Bay Ridge. Our neighborhood included many Italian American families, but only one neighbor had ever heard of a dessert that was similar to schkatalata. Rather, almost every Italian family made struffoli, which are small balls of fried dough with honey, a very popular Christmas treat.

Even when I became an adult and embarked beyond my Brooklyn world, I never met a soul who was familiar with this recipe. Schkatalata, to the exclusion of Grandma Sue and my family, seemed to be obscure.

Yet, every December, Grandma Sue, my mom, my sister, and I prepared hundreds of schkatalata to share with family and friends and also for our own Christmas table. To make this pastry-like treat, Grandma Sue formed a rich dough from three ingredients, flour, muscatel wine, and warm olive oil. We shaped the strips of dough into pinwheels and fried them to a crisp. The pinwheels were then fried again in a deeply intriguing mixture of sweet honey and homemade raisin wine, traditionally called *vine cotte*. Once the schkatalata were done, they were sprinkled with a dusting of warm toasted nuts. This dessert is beyond divine, and it is worth the time just to taste the balance of wine, honey, and raisins with the richness of the dough and the warm, crunchy nuts.

Dear Grandma Sue passed away the day after Christmas in 1983, but her recipe for schkatalata remained with us, and we continued the tradition that had become a strong part of our holiday season. As my mom entered her own senior years, she would have

 her grandchildren around the table, assembly style, shaping the little wheels while she kneaded more and more dough.

With the dawn of the Internet, I sought others throughout the country who make this dessert. I tried every variation that I could think of in the spelling of the name according to Grandma Sue's pronunciation. I could not find it at all, and so I just let my quest for more knowledge about schkatalata rest on the side.

Then one day, years later, a dear friend of mine, Jeanne Lorusso, who lives in California, sent her local farmers' market newsletter to me here in New York. I was taken by complete surprise upon looking at the front cover. The picture showed a huge tray of Grandma Sue's schkatalata, and underneath it read "Cartellate." Bingo! I had found them!

I immediately went online and typed the word "cartellate" into the search engine. Endless websites and a plethora of information came out about Grandma Sue's schkatalata, which, of course, had now been rechristened as cartellate!

All the pictures looked exactly like our little honey-and-raisin wheels. The recipe dates back to the early seventeen hundreds and was proudly made in the Catholic convents of Italy. I also discovered that this is the prime dessert of an area in Italy called Puglia. If one were to stroll the streets of Puglia, they would find Grandma Sue's schkatalata in the windows of local bakeries. This was interesting because Grandma Sue was not from this area of Italy, or even near it.

Upon reading more, I saw that not every recipe for cartellate is exactly the same. Many Americans of Italian descent prepare them with a touch of cinnamon. Others use the juice of figs or prunes. It was noted that Italian nobility would use tangerine juice throughout the centuries, as it was more costly than fig or raisin juice. But all the web sites stated how this dessert is extraordinarily unique in flavor.

Cartellate is the kind of dessert that stirs our memories and allows us to recall the best moments of the holidays during our formative years. Thank you, Grandma Sue. I miss you.

Cartellate

3 $^1/_3$ cup flour

3/4 cup olive oil

3/4 cup muscatel wine

1/4 cup water

1 egg white

Vegetable oil for frying

1 cup vine cotte (recipe to follow)

3/4 cup honey

1/2 cup walnuts

1/2 cup almonds

On a clean work surface, form the flour into the circular shape of a wreath. Heat the olive oil until warm. Sprinkle it along the top of the wreath of flour. With a spoon, mix the oil into the flour until the texture becomes crumbly. Heat the muscatel wine until warm and repeat the process of stirring into the flour. Sprinkle in the water. Knead the flour mixture until it becomes a ball of dough. Wrap the dough in plastic wrap and allow setting for ten minutes.

Cut off a large handful portion of the dough. Take the first piece, dust with a bit of flour, and roll out thinly with a rolling pin. You can also use a pasta machine. Using a fluted-edge pastry cutter, cut the rolled-out dough into 1$^1/_2$"-wide strips. Dip your finger into the egg white and use it as a paste to pinch the dough together about one inch apart along the strip in order to create small boat-like pockets. Bring the dough around from one end and roll the strip to form a rosette. Repeat with remaining strips of dough. Place the cartellate on paper towels overnight in a cool room. The next day they should be a bit stiff.

In a sauté pan, warm vegetable oil over medium heat. Fry a few cartellate at a time, turning over once, until they are golden. In another sauté pan, warm the vine cotte and honey over medium heat. Place the fried cartellate in the warmed mixture for three minutes on each side, or until they are coated well. Layer the walnuts and pecans on a baking sheet and toast until golden brown. Place them in a food processor and pulse lightly until coarse. Arrange the cartellate on a platter and dust with the toasted nuts.

Vine Cotte

1-pound box of raisins
1¹/₂ quarts of water
1 cup sugar

Add raisins to the water and bring to a boil. Simmer, stirring occasionally, over medium-low heat for one hour or until raisins start to plump and burst. Remove the raisins from the water with a slotted spoon. Reserve raisin water in the pot.

Place the raisins, a large spoonful at a time, into a cheesecloth and squeeze the juice out of them through the cloth and back into the pot. Discard the squeezed-out pulp inside the cheesecloth.

When all the raisins are squeezed out through the cheesecloth, add the sugar to the pot. Simmer for one hour and a half or until syrupy. Pour the vine cotte in a jar and cover when cooled. Refrigerate for up to three months.

Anthony and the Lobster Rebellion

A summer getaway to the New Jersey Shore is a favorite pastime for my family. Relaxing days in a lovely beach house, right on the water, are a great way to enjoy each other's company and share heady meals.

For me, cooking up a fresh seafood dinner to go along with the coastal spirit of the getaway begins with a simple walk down the road to the local fishmonger. Upon my return, everyone knows it is time for red lobster sauce with linguine. And always, when I make this sauce, my brother, Anthony, dramatically tells the story of "The Lobster Rebellion."

From my parents, right down to the youngest grandchild, this is a story that we have come to anticipate well. We also know that lobster is a costly luxury, thus the reason for my brother's entertaining recital as part of the lobster dinner. As you will read, Anthony's tale highlights a certain irony.

First, picture a large table with an enthused family of three generations enjoying bowls of linguine topped with a robust, velvety red tomato sauce laced with the incomparable flavor of lobster. On the table are platters of enticing lobsters about to be cracked and consumed with great appreciation of the sweet, moist lobster meat popping out of the shells.

Anthony's story begins in the pre-Revolutionary era. He tells of a prison facility in New England where the lobsters were so abundant that they would crawl all over the shore. The prisoners were served lobster three times daily, seven days a week. They also worked the soil and used lobsters as fertilizer. Suffice to say, most of their world was lobster each and every day.

My brother continues his wild tale of how the prisoners were enraged and would not stand for such treatment. They organized a prison revolt because they never wanted to eat another lobster for the rest of their lives. Anthony never does tell the ending to the story, whether the prisoners ever receive the right to eat a different type of food. He simply wants us to assume whatever conclusion we may imagine.

So, as we are all enjoying the succulent taste of the lobster sauce, we are also envisioning a group of angry men jumping up and down on tables and chairs in a prison cafeteria. They never want to eat another bite of what we are currently enjoying so immensely.

When I sat down to write this chapter, I called my brother at his office. "Tell me all the details of that lobster story. I want to include it in my book."

My brother laughed. "I have no idea if it is even factually correct!"

My brother went on to tell me that his friend Frank Kazeroid told him a version of the story many years ago, obviously trying to convey the same message. I sat there visualizing Frank, Anthony, and their colleagues enjoying an expensive lobster dinner, perhaps in some upscale New York City restaurant, while Frank told of disgruntled New England prisoners forced to eat lobster.

My brother promised to phone Frank and ask him to recall his version of "The Lobster Rebellion." Well, here is what Frank told us: During the Middle Ages and Renaissance, people appreciated lobster. However, modern Europeans and Americans did not hold this crustacean as a popular item. Along the northeastern coast of the United States, the lobster was so common in the seventeenth and eighteenth centuries that it was considered a "junk" food. When caught in great quantities or stranded on shore after severe storms, lobsters served as garden fertilizer and as a food staple given to widows, orphans, indentured servants, and especially prisoners. It was plentiful and cheap, and used in place of proteins that were of more value, so much so that a group of Massachusetts servants decided to take a stand and do something about the situation. They took their owners to court and won a judgment that lobster not be served to them more than three times a week. Eventually, Massachusetts passed a law forbidding its use more than twice a week, citing that a daily lobster dinner was considered cruel and unusual punishment.

The good news is that my linguine with lobster sauce is the opposite. For our family, it is forever linked to warm family vacation dinners on the shore and my brother Anthony's memorable tale of "The Lobster Rebellion."

Lobster Sauce

My lobster sauce recipe boldly calls for a long simmer. This is against the rules and laws of seafood cooking because shellfish will become tough if cooked for a long duration of time. However, in my long experience, I have found that it is ok to go against standard cooking rules as long as one has a tested strategy that yields success. Rather than cooking the whole lobster in the sauce, I opt to cook only the upper body, legs and claws. The tail of the lobster has a great amount of meat that will surely toughen upon a long simmer. Have your fishmonger cut the tails away from the lobster. You can use them for a recipe where they can be stuffed and baked with a filling of your choice or even steamed and enjoyed with clarified butter. The small amounts of meat inside the upper body, legs and claws will remain sweetly moist, and the taste of your sauce may possibly go down in the memory of your guests as the best they ever tasted.

3/4 cup extra-virgin olive oil

1/8 teaspoon crushed red pepper flakes

3 fresh lobsters, each about 1 $^1/_2$ pounds (tails removed)

8 garlic cloves, peeled and crushed

3/4 cup dry white wine

3 28-ounce cans crushed tomatoes

Kosher salt and freshly ground black pepper

Fresh flat-leaf parsley, chopped

In a large pot, warm olive oil over medium heat. Sprinkle in the crushed red pepper flakes and allow to sizzle and flavor the oil. Add the lobster pieces and cook until bright red, about ten minutes. Mix garlic to the lobster and toss about in the oil. Pour the wine, and allow the liquid to evaporate. Add the crushed tomatoes, salt and pepper. Simmer, stirring occasionally, over medium-low heat for two hours. Serve the lobster sauce over linguine or spaghetti and sprinkle with parsley. Arrange lobster pieces on platters for cracking.

Camille's Tip: We never want to waste that scrumptious meat in the thin legs of the lobster. After the lobster is cooked, flatten out the legs and roll over them with a rolling pin. The lobster meat will slip right out.

Jenelle's 9/11 Bus Ride

In September of 2001, I spent some time working away from the culinary world, and instead worked in the financial district of lower Manhattan, better known as the Wall Street area. I was employed by A.G. Edwards and Sons, and I was privileged to work among many fine colleagues.

On the morning of September 11, the infamous day when our country experienced terror attacks on our own soil, those of us who had already arrived at work watched in horror from our office windows after that first plane hit the tower in the World Trade Center. Our building was only a few blocks away, and our own office was located on the top floor, with huge windows covering almost the whole length of the wall. Terribly enough, the view we had was more stark than any cinema screen, more live than any television set, more clear than any photograph. As the second plane hit and did its grave and devastating damage, the screams in our office were deafening and shrill with the astounding terror that the unbelievable had truly occurred. We quickly evacuated and proceeded to live a day that will always remain in our lives and one we will someday recall to our grandchildren.

That evening at home, I realized that I had not seen Jenelle, a dear friend and coworker, at all that day. Jenelle was a strikingly beautiful young woman who was always on time for work and never missed a day. I was very worried, but luckily, I learned that Jenelle had reached her home safely.

Later, she told me her story of that morning. It is really a simple story, but to me, it is so very poignant. Jenelle lived in the borough of Staten Island and traveled into Manhattan each day via the transit express bus through the Brooklyn-Battery Tunnel. That morning, Jenelle was seated at the window, and her bus was still in the tunnel when the tragedy occurred. Due to this, the buses in the tunnel all remained on their spots while the neighboring lane was cleared in order for the many fire engines to quickly pass through to the World Trade Center. Jenelle told me that as the engines passed by her, she gently waved and smiled to the firefighters in encouragement. Many of them waved back appreciatively.

That day, 343 brave New York City firefighters perished. Many were those who passed through the tunnel that morning into Manhattan. For the brave firefighters who waved back at Jenelle and who, within the next hour, saw so much ugliness, her face was something pure for their view, and for many of them, her angelic face was the last beautiful thing they ever saw in this life. Of all the many events and stories that occurred that day, this image will always remain on my mind.

The events of September 11 changed many an attitude in our office on that top floor of our New York City skyscraper. Although we worked in an atmosphere of serious finance, we now all vowed to live office life to the fullest, and a parade of food quickly entered onto the scene. We celebrated every occasion— holidays, bridal showers, newborn babies, birthdays, and retirements. It was a constant party, and we made work a pleasure.

Of course, I was the one to greatly involve food in our celebrations, and I encouraged everyone else to indulge along with me. Our team quickly formed a foodship circle inspired by our shared 9/11 experience. Everyone would bring a special dish to enjoy, and it made our time together as coworkers all the more rich. We would set out a long table of platters piled high with food from each person's home kitchen. We enjoyed the flavors and aromas of such dishes as zesty paella and ceviche, hearty ribs, crunchy country fried chicken, earthy salads, and a variety of homemade baking, which included fresh chocolate cookies, sweet cakes, and breads. I always included my special tiramisu and carrot cake. Yes, our office was a bountiful smorgasbord.

Eventually, Jenelle married Alfonso, a terrific young man from Ecuador. This was my first introduction to Ecuadorian cuisine. Jenelle would always tell me about her visits to restaurants in New York City that served authentic Ecuadorian dishes, and she would describe the enticing ingredients that Alfonso's family used in their cooking. Jenelle's favorite Ecuadorian recipe is seafood ceviche. I am happy to pass it on.

Seafood Ceviche

2 tablespoons red onion, cut into thin semicircular slices

2 tablespoons sea salt

3 cups boiled medium shrimp, peeled and deveined

1 cup corn kernels

2 medium tomatoes, chopped

2 tablespoons fresh-squeezed lime juice

1/4 cup fresh-squeezed orange juice

1/2 cup ketchup

1 tablespoon mustard

1 tablespoon white vinegar

1 tablespoon raw sugar

2 tablespoons fresh cilantro, chopped

Place the red onions in a cup of water, and add sea salt. Soak for fifteen minutes. Drain, and gently rinse with water. Mix onions, shrimp, corn, and tomatoes in a large bowl. Whisk together lime juice, orange juice, ketchup, mustard, white vinegar, and raw sugar in a separate bowl, and then stir into shrimp mixture. Sprinkle with cilantro and allow the acidic juices to settle as the flavors combine. Serve in chilled glasses.

Jenny's Place

One of the greatest things about our country is how any individual can engage in free enterprise, exhibit one's talents, be among the community, and of course, share one's own signature food and recipes. This combination has always been my particular favorite, and it always brings my friend Jenny to mind.

I first met Jenny when I was networking for the nonprofit organization I preside over in support of childhood cancer. As I made my rounds, I came across a brand-new Mexican restaurant. The establishment was small, but very inviting, decorated in a bright, charming fashion, and held promise that gratifying dishes would emerge from the kitchen.

The owner was Jenny. She introduced herself and explained that she was new to the community. I immediately found her to be a warm and unique person. She is of Asian descent, yet an expert on Spanish and Mexican cuisine. The concept of her restaurant is to serve fresh, wholesome ingredients made without additives and minus pork.

As Jenny was new to the area, she was unfamiliar with our elected officials, community leaders, and local newspapers. She clearly demonstrated a strong work ethic, and she had such an eager ambition. This motivated me to help her on the path toward success. I gave her advice based on my own years as a restaurateur, and I suggested a grand opening in order to introduce her and her new endeavor to the community.

The night of the grand opening went very well, and Jenny's amazing food was the star, especially her guacamole, which is the best I have ever tasted. She also served piping-hot burritos with creamy Mexican cheeses and spices. Jenny had high hopes that her new business would pick up. I reassured her that as people learned of her establishment, they would not be able to resist her delectable offerings. I left that evening with a special prayer and positive thoughts for her success.

Months passed by, and I had been absent from Jenny's restaurant for a while and missed her and her gratifying Mexican food. Then, one Friday night, I was driving home after a long day and with no thoughts about what to prepare for dinner. I called my youngest son, Christopher, who was at a sporting event. He would not be home until later in the evening, but he had a craving for

 Jenny's guacamole as a late-night snack when he returned. I was only a few blocks from Jenny's restaurant, and since I was overdue a visit, I parked and went in to pick up my son's guacamole and also to say hi to my friend.

What I found at the entrance of Jenny's restaurant was thrilling. There was a long line of patrons waiting to be seated! I entered and waved to Jenny, who was running all over, serving her customers. To me, this completely spelled success.

However, Jenny was missing two waiters that night, as well as her helper who was in charge of deliveries at the takeout area. She grabbed me by the hand and asked me to hurry and pick up the phone that was ringing and ringing for takeout orders. As happy as I was to see Jenny's restaurant bustling with such energetic activity, I went into serious business mode and galvanized myself into action.

That evening I stayed for the whole night shift. It had been years since I had owned my own restaurant with my ex-husband, but it all came back to me on just how to proceed. Jenny and I worked side by side with her busboys and deliverymen. We took orders, served, packed food, cleaned off tables, and ensured that every last customer enjoyed a satisfying visit.

When the evening came to an end, Jenny and I, exhausted, sat down together in the empty dining room to laugh and enjoy a well-deserved sangria. We toasted to our friendship and to the success that was now hers. I recalled the first time I met her when she had been so hopeful and eager to make this happen. It did happen, and I was so happy to have my own very small part in the adventure. For me, this is a proud foodship.

When it was time to go home, I left with a generous order of Jennie's guacamole. The trick to excellent guacamole is to make sure the flavor of the avocado is not overpowered by the other ingredients. The onions and tomatoes and all else should just enhance the flavor of the avocado. Jenny's is superb, and I thank her for sharing her recipe.

Jenny's Guacamole

3 small avocados, halved and scooped

1 tablespoon fresh-squeezed lime juice

1 small onion, diced

1 Roma tomato, diced

1 tablespoon fresh cilantro, chopped

Kosher salt and freshly ground black pepper

Scoop the avocado from the shells and cut into pieces. Place in a bowl and toss with lime juice. Gently mash the avocado, and then add the onions, Roma tomatoes, cilantro, salt, and pepper. Serve chilled with nachos.

Uncle Sammy and His Secret Marinara Sauce

In the "old neighborhood," where my mom grew up, the men were all considered the most charming of men and Uncle Sammy Trimboli was no exception. My mother's sister, my aunt Mary, was married to Stevie, Sammy's brother, and my cousins would speak about their uncle Sammy's extraordinary talent for cooking and, most especially, his secret marinara sauce.

But first, a few words about the old neighborhood. My grandparents, Grandpa Luigi and Grandma Carmela, lived in the Park Slope section of Brooklyn back in the early to mid-nineteen hundreds. During that time, this area of Brooklyn was very populated with Italian immigrants. As the decades went by, their children and grandchildren grew older and moved away to the suburbs of New York and New Jersey. But for the space of time in between the landing of so many Italians on American soil and the movement toward suburbia, there was a quaint old-world community of faith, food, and togetherness. I consider this a very golden period in the history of Italian New York.

It was during this time that the seeds were planted for what would become the legendary fame of Uncle Sammy's "secret marinara sauce." Uncle Sammy was the owner of a popular neighborhood tavern. He was the chef extraordinaire, and his own uncle was the master of ceremonies on a continual basis, always hosting dozens of friends at a time to taste Uncle Sammy's outstanding cooking.

When I asked Johnny, Uncle Sammy's son, about his dad's menu, he told me that his father did not have one! Rather, Uncle Sammy cooked whatever would best please their many guests, or simply to suit however the creative juices flowed that day. He cooked for dozens and dozens of guests nightly, and he did this in a small kitchen downstairs in the establishment. Johnny recalls that the kitchen could not have been more than ten by five, and if one were to ask Uncle Sammy for one of his remarkable recipes, he would find it difficult to actually recite one. This was because he cooked "by eye" and with a flourished talent that did not determine exact amounts.

Johnny also told me, at length, of how his father's tavern was host to some of the greatest names in the entertainment and sports world after World War II. Many found their way to Uncle Sammy's tavern, such as Jimmy Durante, Jerry Vale, Jack Dempsey, and Jimmy Roselli. Jimmy Durante would finish entertaining at the famous Paramount Theatre in Manhattan and then inform the many fans and theatergoers that he was now on his way to Brooklyn for the best marinara sauce in New York City. When he arrived, he would play at the piano while everyone gathered around to enjoy good music along with good food.

For four decades, Uncle Sammy cooked and bartended, and always more and more people wanted his special marinara sauce with the secret ingredient. Every Christmas season, he simmered countless pots of sauce to keep up with the demand of so many who wanted tremendous gallon jars for their own Christmas feast. Uncle

Sammy did not really "sell" the sauce. He simply made it, and everyone would come into the tavern asking for it. In their gratitude, they would hand him any amount of money, sometimes as high as a hundred dollars, or maybe a bottle of wine or spirits, and Uncle Sammy would happily share his sauce with one and all, wishing them a Merry Christmas.

Years later, when Uncle Sammy passed away, Johnny had two frozen containers of the last pot of sauce that Uncle Sammy had prepared at the very end of his life. It was shared at the table among their family, and Johnny recalls it as a very special meal.

Since then, Uncle Sammy's family has prepared the sauce, always trying to recapture his magical flavor of years gone by. Johnny told me of a recent summer weekend when he hosted a barbecue in his backyard for family and friends. He was determined, more than ever, to prepare the sauce and yield the exact taste his father would serve. When he presented the sauce and pasta, it was Johnny's nephew who saluted him, stating that the sauce was as close to Grandpa's as he could ever imagine tasting again. Johnny was completely touched, and he realized that his father was not gone at all, but still truly here. This is the foodship that Uncle Sammy left behind for his family.

During the writing of this book, my uncle Stevie, Sammy's brother, passed away at the age of ninety-five. It was then that I had an opportunity to see Johnny after not seeing him for quite a few years. He is a talented gourmet himself, as well as a past restaurant owner. With a twinkle in his eye, and with his father's charm, he asked me if I would like to include the recipe for his father's secret marinara sauce.

To say that I was elated is an understatement! Johnny explained that his father's recipe, although a "secret," was meant to be shared with warmth and love so that as many people as possible could enjoy it in the future years ahead, just as so many enjoyed it during Uncle Sammy's lifetime in the past. Johnny also uncovered the special ingredient of his father's sauce, cream sherry.

Thank you, Johnny, and thank you, Uncle Sammy.

Uncle Sammy's Marinara Sauce

1/2 cup extra-virgin olive oil

One medium onion, diced

3 garlic cloves, peeled and sliced

2 28-ounce cans whole skinless tomatoes, strained

2 tablespoons table salt

Freshly ground pepper, to taste

1/2 cup packed fresh basil, chopped

1/3 cup cream sherry

In a large pot, warm olive oil over medium heat. Add onions and allow to cook until translucent. Add garlic and cook until tender. Stir in tomatoes, salt, pepper, basil, and cream sherry. Reduce heat to low and simmer for an hour and a half. Serve over pasta, and top with a high quality grated cheese such as Parmigiano-Reggiano.

Ray Ewen and Padre Pio

As a Roman Catholic, I have a special devotion to Padre Pio, a modern-day saint who was born in the late eighteen hundreds and died in 1963. He bore the stigmata of Christ, and I, for one, have always found this fascinating.

The town of Barto, Pennsylvania, is the home of the National Shrine of Padre Pio, and on September 23, the special feast day of this saint, many people travel to visit the shrine. One year, my sons and I made the trip from New York City. During this time, my oldest son, Frankie, had just entered into remission from cancer. On that day, a special guest speaker was present. His name was Ray Ewen.

Ray was a World War II vet, and a personal friend of Padre Pio during his lifetime. Ray stood at the podium and told of his remarkable experiences with this historical religious figure. During their time in knowing each other, Padre Pio was a Capuchin friar in a small town in the south of Italy called Pietrelcina. Ray was an American soldier in the Air Force who would often travel there to meet the mystical friar who so many people spoke of with such reverence.

When Ray addressed the faithful with his stories, many were greatly mesmerized by his firsthand account of knowing a saint who had been physically touched by Christ. That day, when my sons and I first heard Ray speak, was no different.

When Ray was finished, Frankie, who had prayed a great

deal to Padre Pio, was very impressed. He said, "Mom, I must meet that man!"

Many people were in line to greet Ray and shake his hand. Upon my son's turn, Ray became quiet for a moment. During my son's cancer battle, part of his treatment was a full leg amputation. That day, our car ride to Pennsylvania from New York City was a long one, and so Frankie had opted not to wear his prosthesis. There my son stood, on his crutches, and his hair, eyelashes, and eyebrows had not grown back just yet from the chemotherapy treatments.

Ray looked down and saw my son's missing leg. Then he looked back up at his face and smiled gently in realization. Ray's eyes lightly teared as he asked, "Son, will you pray the Hail Mary with me?"
My son said, "Yes, sir."

As my sixteen-year-old son leaned on his crutches, he reached out and locked both hands with this eighty-eight-year-old World War II vet, and together, they prayed deeply in unison. Watching them, it was one of the most profound moments of my life.

In the time following, Ray became a dear friend. He prayed for my son daily, with rosary beads that had been blessed by Padre Pio. I had an opportunity to visit him and share more of his life. Ray's home was one of wonder. He held many relics and spiritual possessions that reflected his sterling life and love of God. Visits with Ray were wonderful times where we would sit and have coffee along with the special cookies I would bring. I was very interested in Ray's German heritage and its cooking. To my delight, his family shared a very special recipe that they had enjoyed for many years, apple cake. Ray's granddaughter, Christine, explained that Ray's late wife would bake this on happy occasions. I am so pleased to have this recipe. It brings back stirring memories of my time in knowing Ray.

Ewen Family Apple Cake

3 apples, peeled, cored, and sliced to ¼-inch thickness

2 cups, plus 5 tablespoons of sugar

2 teaspoons ground cinnamon

3 cups flour

4 eggs

3 teaspoons baking powder

1/2 teaspoon salt

1 cup vegetable oil

1/2 cup orange juice

$2^1/_2$ teaspoons vanilla extract

Sprinkle sliced apples with the five tablespoons of white sugar and the ground cinnamon. In a large bowl, mix the flour, eggs, two cups sugar, baking powder, salt, vegetable oil, orange juice, and vanilla until well blended. Pour half of the batter into a prepared greased baking pan. Place the apple mixture over the batter, and then pour the remaining batter over the top. Bake in a preheated oven at 350°F for one hour and ten minutes. Let cake cool in pan.

Camille's Tip: When baking with apples, it is best to use Cortland, Empire, or Golden Delicious. All three varieties will maintain their shape during the baking process.

The Eggplant Parmigiana Connection

My grandmother Carmela, my mom's mom, spent a great part of her kitchen life frying eggplants in readiness to be made into the age-old crowd-pleasing casserole-type fare.

Grandma Carmela was a mother to eight children. My mom was her youngest, and my aunt Pauline, whom I write about in this book, was her oldest child. How I wish I could write that I knew my grandmother Carmela. I did not, and although only half of her many grandchildren knew her, still her legacy lives strong and well in our family. She was a beautiful woman who loved fine living. She kept a lovely and immaculate home. She valued quality fashion in her clothing and home decor, and of course, she was an excellent cook. She passed down many recipes to her children, especially her four daughters, who, in turn, have passed them down to my generation.

In the nineteen thirties and forties, my grandfather Luigi worked in the giant-sized fruit and vegetable markets in Manhattan. He worked nights, and so his "dinner" meal was early in the morning. Grandma Carmela would prepare oatmeal, pancakes, and sunny-side eggs for her children while cooking up steaks, pasta, vegetables, cutlets, and soups for her husband. At night, she repeated dinner again for her children. Suffice it to say, my grandmother, when not cleaning, was always cooking.

Of all my grandmother's many recipes, her eggplant parmigiana stands out. When my aunt Mary, my grandmother's middle daughter, was engaged to be married, my grandparents hosted a house party in their home in the Park Slope section of Brooklyn, and they invited almost a hundred people.

In the following years, the story was told and retold how the many guests crowded the front yard and the backyard. They sat along the stairs leading to the second floor of Grandma Carmela's home. They filled the living room, dining room, and my grandmother's kitchen. And in the days leading up to the event, my grandmother, along with her own sisters, fried countless eggplants so that her special dish could be served.

Grandma would fry each shiny purple eggplant round to an extra crisp. The layers of the dish held more than one fresh type of cheese, which melted so well with the red tomato sauce. Served piping hot, the flavor was like an Italian summer garden.

Years later, when I became a mother, I would think of my grandmother often when preparing her eggplant recipe with my son Nicky. Nicky is my second child, and a young adult with autism.

I have always felt that simple food preparation is a terrific therapeutic tool for children and adults with autism. Although Nicky is nonverbal, food is a true communicator for him. Some of my quietest, and most enchanting moments in my kitchen are when Nicky and I prepare my grandmother Carmela's eggplant parmigiana. I carefully show him how to layer the eggplant, spoon the sauce, and sprinkle the cheese. Slowly and productively, and with some prompting, my son accomplishes quite a pan of eggplant. When the finished product is in front of us on the kitchen table, we both have a great sense of satisfaction.

As I think of my grandmother, I wonder what she would have thought, as she made her own countless pans of eggplant parmigiana over the years, if she could know that her granddaughter, decades later, would teach her special-needs child this timeless preparation of such a simple dish. I am sure she would have been proud, and I know I am proud to have this as one of my favorite foodships.

Eggplant Parmigiana

2 large eggplants

1 cup flour

3 eggs, beaten

2 cups seasoned bread crumbs

Vegetable oil for frying

Marinara sauce (page 227)

1 pound mozzarella cheese, sliced about 1/8-inch thick

2 cups Parmigiano-Reggiano cheese, grated

Remove skin from the eggplant with a peeler and cut into quarter-inch thick slices. Prepare three shallow dishes each for the flour, beaten eggs, and bread crumbs. Coat each side of the eggplant with the flour, shaking off any excess, then dip in the eggs, and then in the bread crumbs. In a sauté pan, warm vegetable oil over medium heat. Add the eggplant pieces, a few at a time, and fry until golden, turning over once. In a rectangular baking pan, layer the ingredients, starting with a generous amount of marinara sauce on the bottom of the pan, then the eggplant, more sauce, and then fresh mozzarella and Parmigiano–Reggiano cheese. Continue to layer until you reach the top of the pan. In a preheated oven, bake at 350°F for thirty minutes, until bubbly.

Bob the Beautifier

I met Bob on the day my son passed away. Frankie had been in hospice at home, and I would not leave his bedside for a moment. All those around me were very worried because I was hardly eating, drinking, or sleeping. My family and friends encouraged me to take a break for a few moments, but of course, I would not listen to their pleas.

A block away from my home, there was a new salon owner, Bob. Although he was in such close proximity to me, I was unaware of his presence because I had spent the last two years in and out of the hospital with my son. My niece, Christina, in desperation, went to see Bob, and she introduced herself. She explained to him that her aunt needed to take a break for at least an hour in order to recharge herself. She asked Bob if he would come to our home and do my hair, which by now had inches of gray roots. He had many customers and was unable to leave his salon, but he told my niece to bring me to see him and he would do my hair as quick as possible.

When Christina returned and relayed this message, I refused to go to Bob's salon. The very idea! However, after much pleading by her and two close friends, Sandra and Maria, I finally relented, and the four of us went to Bob's salon. Bob quickly applied the dye. He was very quiet and kind as he finished my hair. I thanked him and quickly returned to my son. That evening, my son passed on to that better place.

Early the next morning, the doorbell of my home rang. It

was a very different ring from the usual sound. This time it sounded like church bells. I went to the door, and nobody was there. This has continued to happen at many random times since my son died, and frankly, it is much unexplained.

Eventually, about a month after Frankie left us, I went to visit Bob and asked him if he remembered me. He said that he could never forget the day he met me, and he was very glad I had returned. He expressed his condolences, and as we were talking, the bell to the glass door of his salon shop rang. It was the same exact sound as the church bells in my home, and to my astonishment, nobody was at the door of his salon. Stunned, I asked Bob if that had ever occurred before. He told me that it had started about a month ago. I asked him if it started around the time he met me. In realization, he said yes, it did.

Since then I have become one of Bob's best customers. We have grown a fine friendship, and the bell still chimes as a church bell in his salon, just as it does in my home. As I have grown in my grief and helped myself to move on, Bob has been there for me. As I wrote this book, I would tell Bob about every step of the way. And many times as I would sit in the salon chair, while Bob worked his magic on my hair, the bell would ring and nobody would be at the door.

Bob, who never believed in mystical experiences from the other side, now reflects and contemplates on this special connection of our mutual ringing doorbells and our friendship that began the day my son passed away. Sometimes when the bell rings, we will laugh, and he will say, "Okay, Camille, time to talk about food!"

For every holiday, party, and event that I host, I will sit in Bob's chair, and he will want to know all the details of the meal I am planning. I tell Bob of all the different recipes and ingredients as he happily works on my hair. Of course, I often ask Bob of his own culture and food. Bob is from Israel, and he tells me of the Jewish recipes his mother and wife prepare for family and friends.

Other than our ringing doorbells, Bob and I also share a

guilty love of dishes heavy in carbohydrates and cholesterol. The one that Bob taught me, a cheesy potato casserole, is so ambrosial and so high in calories that I actually feel like I am sinning when I eat it! But the taste is very worth it, as long as we serve it on occasion and not to the norm. When Bob gave me this recipe, I asked him if this is

his version of a kugel, which, in Jewish cooking, is a traditional egg noodle or potato pudding. He told me that this is simply his very own cheesy potato casserole, but I can consider it kugel if I like.

One more thing, the very first time I made Bob's cheesy potato casserole, the doorbell rang in my home.

Cheesy Potato Casserole

5 medium potatoes, peeled and parboiled

Kosher salt and freshly ground black pepper

12 ounces heavy cream

Vegetable oil

4 cups button mushrooms, sliced

1/2 pound Swiss cheese

Cut potatoes into slices and layer in a buttered baking dish. Season with salt and pepper. Bring heavy cream to a boil and pour over the potatoes. In a sauté pan, over medium heat, warm vegetable oil and give mushrooms a quick fry. Layer mushrooms over the potatoes and heavy cream. Bake in a preheated oven at 400°F for twenty-five minutes. Layer slices of Swiss cheese to cover the mushrooms and potatoes completely. Bake an additional ten minutes, until melted and bubbly. Allow to settle for five minutes before serving.

Chef Enzo and His Daughter

For many years, my family and I would frequent a restaurant in Brooklyn called Ponte Vecchio. The atmosphere had a cool, sophisticated Italian charm, and the food was unsurpassed.

One of the owners of Ponte Vecchio is a chef named Enzo, and he is a skilled master in the kitchen, having been professionally trained in Italy and cooking from the time he was fourteen years old. As a young man, Enzo was a chef on the Italian SS *Michelangelo*. When he arrived in the United States, he worked on the famous Mulberry Street in the Little Italy section of New York City. He eventually achieved his dream of owning his own restaurant, and as of this writing, he has owned Ponte Vecchio for thirty-five years.

Although I have been dining at Enzo's establishment since my very young teen years, I never knew that he and I share a common bond. We are both parents of a special-needs child. When I was almost at the very end stages of writing this book, I was out to dinner with family and friends at Ponte Vecchio. Enzo came over to our table to greet us. We exchanged cordial chat, and he started to talk about his daughter, who is severely challenged in her mental development. Enzo told me of his journey in raising his daughter, who is now a young adult. The greatest challenge is that his daughter does not speak or recognize others with any familiarity, not even her parents. Enzo's demeanor was very solemn when he shared this with me.

However, suddenly a spark came into his eyes as he spoke.

He said, "But you know, there is one time, the only time, when my daughter and I connect and when I know that she understands that I am her father. And that is when I cook for her."

Enzo went on to tell how he uses food to share moments with his daughter that they otherwise might not experience together. I asked Enzo about his daughter's favorite foods. He told me that she enjoys bright colors on her plate, and he would start a meal off for her with an appetizer of sweet melon, fresh tomato, and prosciutto. She especially loves fresh fruits with his homemade cold whipped cream on summer days, and in the mornings, he will prepare a fluffy potato frittata with sausages.

I told him, "Enzo, I *must* write about you in my cookbook. You and your daughter are amazing, and you very much reflect the message that I wish to share with my future readers."

Enzo generously shared two recipes with me. The first is one of his gourmet creations that is a best seller at his restaurant, bucatini puttanesca.

Enzo's second recipe is for filet of sole and calls for just a few ingredients. This allows the natural fresh taste of the fish to shine. It is a simple dish such as this that Enzo prepares, with love, for his daughter. She always gifts him back with a bright smile on her face. What an amazing foodship.

Bucatini Puttanesca

1 pound bucatini pasta

6 tablespoons extra-virgin olive oil

4 garlic cloves, peeled and chopped

20 Gaeta olives

2 tablespoons capers

1 teaspoon oregano

1 24 ounce can San Marzano whole tomatoes

Sea salt and freshly ground black pepper

1 tablespoon parsley, chopped

5 leaves of basil

In a large pot, boil water for the bucatini. When water begins to boil, add salt liberally. Let water return to a boil. Add bucatini, and cook until al dente. In a large sauté pan, warm olive oil over medium heat. Add garlic, Gaeta olives, capers and oregano. Cook until tender. Pour in San Marzano tomatoes. Crush them into the pan with the back of a spoon. Stir ingredients very well and bring to a quick boil. Sprinkle in salt and pepper. Lower heat and gently simmer for thirty minutes. Add the bucatini and toss well with the pasta. Garnish with parsley and basil.

Chef Enzo's Filet of Sole

2 filets of sole, about 4 ounces each

Kosher salt

4 tablespoons extra-virgin olive oil

2 tablespoons fresh-squeezed lemon juice

2 tablespoons very fine bread crumbs

Season filet of sole with salt. Place in a baking dish. Whisk olive oil and lemon juice. Pour mixture over filets and into the bottom of the baking dish. Sprinkle bread crumbs over the filets. Cover with aluminum foil and bake in preheated oven at 350°F for twelve minutes.

Part Two
Treasures

"Life is a combination of magic and pasta."
~Frederico Fellini

From my early childhood, and along the course of my life, I have been blessed with knowing phenomenal people along the way. Some are my closest relatives. Others are cherished friends, old and new. Each person in this part of my book have a place in my heart for various reasons. To my further happiness, all are connected with a special food. It is my pleasure to share these special people with you along with special recipes.

Aunt Pauline and Uncle Nicky's Seafood Salad

Seafood salad, also called *frutti di mare*, which means "fruit of the sea" in Italian, has long been an anticipated appetizer for many Italian American families, most especially on Christmas Eve, when we celebrate "the Feast of the Seven Fishes."

In my own family, my aunt Pauline and her husband, Nicky, deserve our thanks for handing down their interpretation of this recipe. Aunt Pauline was my mother's oldest sibling of eight children. She and Uncle Nicky never had children of their own, but they were blessed with many nieces and nephews who adored them. They had a joy of life, traveled often, and dined in the finest restaurants. They were also among the most charitable and sincere people I have ever known. I consider my time with them to be one life-long foodship as they shared their lively and vibrant culinary world continually.

Many years ago, when my sister, Lucy, and her husband were newlyweds, they opened an Italian family-style restaurant. Aunt Pauline and Uncle Nicky, who loved to cook together and entertained in grand style in their home, would often visit Lucy at her new establishment. They had a lot of advice and tips on how to serve the most delicious of fare.

Many members of our family worked at the restaurant in order to ensure its success. What fun we all had under the tutelage of our favorite aunt and uncle. A vivid teenage memory of mine was an early Saturday morning when the food was being prepared in readiness for the afternoon lunch crowd. Uncle Nicky announced that the restaurant must serve seafood salad, and that he and Aunt Pauline would teach those in the kitchen how to prepare it to perfection.

I can still recall the plump pink jumbo shrimps, so brilliant among the colorful seafood. Along with black olives and bright yellow lemon wedges, it was all tossed in a fragrant homemade  dressing of extra-virgin olive oil, red pepper flakes, fresh parsley, and crushed garlic.

Of course, the seafood salad was an instant hit among the patrons, and countless dishes were served, as well as orders of catering trays on Christmas Eve.

Aunt Pauline and Uncle Nicky left behind an amazing legacy of family love, laughter, and joy. Those values are especially remembered when I recall them enjoying good food and wine at their large oval-shaped dining room table, surrounded by many family members and friends. Now, decades later, on every Christmas Eve, for the Feast of the Seven Fishes, we all gather to enjoy their recipe for seafood salad as part of our antipasto course. And as for Lucy's restaurant, she still has Aunt Pauline and Uncle Nicky's Seafood Salad on her menu, thirty years later.

Seafood Salad

Dressing

1/4 cup fresh-squeezed lemon juice

2 tablespoons white vinegar

1/2 cup extra-virgin olive oil

2 tablespoons fresh flat-leaf parsley, chopped

Kosher salt and freshly ground black pepper

1/8 teaspoon crushed red pepper flakes

3 garlic cloves, peeled and crushed

Seafood

1/4 pound frozen scungilli (conch meat), defrosted and cleaned

1 small octopus

1/2 pound cleaned calamari, cut into 1/2-inch rings

1 pound medium shrimp, peeled and deveined

1 stalk celery, sliced

1/2 cup commercial black olives, sliced

1 lemon, cut into wedges

2 tablespoons fresh flat-leaf parsley, chopped

In a large bowl, whisk the lemon juice, white vinegar, olive oil, parsley, salt, pepper, and red pepper flakes. Add the crushed garlic. Set the dressing aside and allow to settle while the flavors combine. Bring a large pot of water to boil. Add the scungilli and octopus, and simmer for thirty-five minutes. Allow to cool.

In a smaller pot of boiling water, add the calamari for one and half minutes. With a slotted spoon, remove the calamari into a bowl of ice water to stop the cooking process. Place the shrimp in the same medium pot of boiling water and boil for four minutes. Remove it to the bowl of ice water to stop the cooking process.

When all the seafood is cool enough to handle, prepare each to be part of the salad: Slice the scungilli. Cut the tentacles from the octopus, and cut each tentacle into one-inch pieces. Cut the octopus head into four pieces. Leave calamari in rings, and the shrimps whole. In a large bowl, toss the seafood, celery, olives, lemons and parsley. Chill well and serve.

Aunt Angie with the Cookies

My aunt Angie gained her nickname "Aunt Angie with the Cookies" due to her extraordinary success in mastering the art of baking mountains of outstanding cookies. Married to my mother's brother, Frank, she is, without a doubt, the best home baker I have ever known.

Many decades ago, from the first time Aunt Angie was introduced into my mother's family as a young lady, she was embraced by one and all. My grandmother greatly approved of Aunt Angie's polished good taste, her fine manners, her background of a good family, and her outgoing personality. She and my uncle Frank enjoyed a long and happy marriage, and while raising her son, she held a very high position in upper management in her company. During an era where having women in the workplace was not the ordinary as it is now, this was quite an accomplishment.

Through it all, Aunt Angie baked. She built a reputation among her friends, family, and colleagues for her colorful, moist, fresh cookies and also her cakes, pies, pastries, and breads.

At the time of this writing, Aunt Angie, at the age of ninety-two, told me that her love of baking started as a child. She learned from her grandmother and never stopped baking through her whole life. She was always on a quest for new recipes, and over the years, she would find them wherever they were available, usually magazines or cookbooks. She would bake a recipe and always try to improve on it, re-creating it a bit to make it her own. If it reached her high standard, then it became a dessert that many would enjoy in all the following years.

Every Christmas, we looked forward to Aunt Angie's huge tray of cookies on the holiday table. All different shapes and sizes, and many flavors, including chocolate, coconut, various liqueurs, nuts, and fruits, were all baked in the rich, sugary goodness of fresh butter and snowy flour. She baked a variety of up to twenty different cookies, which were carefully arranged high on the tray. As the decades rolled by, it reached the point where Aunt Angie baked over a thousand cookies every holiday season, using up to fifty pounds of flour. Her trays were shipped out from New York to as far as California, where appreciative family and friends waited eagerly for their annual holiday dessert.

Of all Aunt Angie's cookies, my sons most enjoyed her butter cookies cut into Christmas tree shapes. One warm day in July, my oldest son, Frankie, and my youngest son, Christopher, were talking about those cookies while we were in Frankie's hospital room during his chemo treatments. They were agreeing how neat it would be to have those cookies in the summer instead of waiting until Christmas. My mom, who was happy that Frankie was getting back an appetite, mentioned this to Aunt Angie on the phone that evening. The next day, Aunt Angie's tray of cookies arrived at our hospital room, and it was piled high with that one type of cookie, the Christmas trees! My sons indulged in those cookies and proudly shared them with the doctors and nurses, informing them how their great-aunt is a baker extraordinaire.

As I share Aunt Angie's Christmas tree cookie recipe, I have a vision of her, a senior citizen, lovingly baking those cookies for my sons and sending them off to the hospital so that they could have a sweet taste of Christmas in July.

Christmas Tree Butter Cookies

1 cup butter

1 cup sugar

2 teaspoons vanilla

2 eggs, yolks separated from whites

3 cups flour

1 teaspoon salt

2 teaspoons fresh-squeezed lemon juice

3 cups of confectioners' sugar

Red and green sprinkles

In a large bowl, cream together butter and sugar for three minutes. Add vanilla and egg yolks. Beat until well blended. In a separate bowl, mix flour and salt. Add flour-and-salt mixture, one cup at a time, to the butter mixture. Mix at low speed until a dough forms.

On a floured work surface, roll dough out a quarter inch thick. Cut with a Christmas tree-shaped cookie cutter. Bake in a preheated oven at 375°F for ten to twelve minutes. Cool cookies on rack.

Beat the egg whites with the lemon juice. Add the confectioners' sugar, and mix well until well blended. Spread a thin layer of icing on the cookies and drizzle with red and green sprinkles.

Camille's tips: Icing will harden if not used quickly after preparing. If you are not using immediately, then pour the glaze into an airtight container until you are ready to use on cookies or cake.

Pauline, Mary, Anna, and JoJo

Any part of a book that tells of special people must include one's mother. My mother, who is affectionately called "JoJo" by those who admire and respect her, was a stay-at-home mom in the sixties and seventies. This was an era when many moms did not work outside of the house. Daily, my mother prepared a well-rounded all–American dinner. In addition to the main dish of meat, chicken, pork or fish, her rule was a green vegetable each night, and a "starch," as she called it, usually potatoes, corn, stuffing, or rice. However, on Sundays, she prepared a full Italian-style feast, complete with antipasto, pasta and meat sauce, chicken or veal, and an array of vegetables. This was always followed by chocolate layer cake from Ebinger's Bakery, or cheesecake and pastry from a local Italian bakery.

Holidays were even more festive. My mother had three sisters, Pauline, Mary, and Anna. Mom and my aunts were extremely close, and they always took turns hosting holidays in their homes. However, no matter who was hosting and setting the long table in her dining room, they always helped each other cook the feast in the days leading up to the holiday. The morning of December 24, my mother and I would arrive very early at Aunt Anna's house. Later on in the evening, Aunt Anna would host the Feast of the Seven Fishes for over twenty family members. In many Italian American homes, this grand seafood dinner is a Christmas Eve tradition. Every year of my childhood, and well into my teen years, I would sit from early in the morning with my mother and my three aunts, helping to prepare the many types of seafood to be served to our large family. Always, each year, my aunts would tell of how my grandmother Carmela and her own sisters would prepare this meal every Christmas Eve.

Aunt Mary taught me how to make her special dish of pulpo, which is baby octopus steamed in extra-virgin olive oil and onions. Aunt Pauline taught me how to prepare lobster tails filled with a garlic butter stuffing and baked to a moist crisp. It is no wonder that, as an adult, I always host Christmas Eve dinner in my own home, and every year I think of Aunt Mary when I am preparing the pulpo, and Aunt Pauline when I am filling the lobster tails.

When I talked to my mother about the recipe that she thinks most represents her and her sisters as a team, surprisingly she did not name a seafood dish. Rather, she told me that of all the foods they prepared over the years, everyone always asked them to repeat stuffed red peppers. I wholeheartedly agree. The recipe for our stuffed red peppers was an original recipe passed down from my great-grandmother, Grandmother Carmela's mother, who was named Xaveria. Great Grandma Xaveria's filling is a unique one that yields a peppery bite, combining the warm taste of pine nuts with the sharper flavors of anchovies and capers, filled into a sweet red pepper. This recipe calls for a filling made with whole wheat freselle. Freselle is a doughnut shaped and twice-baked bread originating from Puglia and Calabria and sold here in the United

States. You can purchase freselle in most Italian gourmet shops, but if you can't find it then you may use toasted Italian whole wheat bread.

Stuffed Peppers

4 large red bell peppers

6 rounds of whole wheat freselle or a medium loaf of whole wheat
Italian bread

2 tablespoons olive oil

Oil from jar of anchovies

2 tablespoons toasted pine nuts

2 garlic cloves, peeled and sliced

2 tablespoons capers

1/2 cup black olives, sliced

6 anchovy filets (from jar), with oil

1/8 teaspoon crushed red pepper flakes

2 tablespoons tomato paste

Cut the peppers in half lengthwise. Remove the seeds and white
ribs. Place in a baking pan in readiness to be filled.

Pulse the freselle in a food processor until coarse. If using Italian
bread, slice the loaf and arrange slices on a baking sheet. Toast in
oven at 350°F for ten minutes, turning over once. Pulse the bread in
the food processor until coarse and set aside.

In a large sauté pan, warm the olive oil and oil from the jar of
anchovies over medium heat. Add the pine nuts and allow to cook
until toasty and golden in color. Stir in the garlic, capers, olives,

anchovies, red pepper flakes and tomato paste. Allow to cook on low-to-medium heat for five minutes. Add the freselle crumbs or whole wheat bread crumbs into the pan and stir well until all ingredients and flavors combine. Fill each pepper with the mixture.

Add a quarter of an inch of water to the bottom of the pan, and cover with foil. Bake at 350°F for forty minutes. Remove foil and bake for an additional ten minutes. Push a fork through the pepper to make sure it is tender and fully cooked.

Camille's Tip: When cooking with anchovies, always try to buy the brands that are sold in the jar as opposed to the flat tin cans. Jarred anchovies yield a better flavor and quality.

Grandma Josephine

My paternal grandmother was named Josephine. I am told that she was a charming woman with a constant smile on her face and a soft and sweet disposition in every avenue of her life. Grandma Josephine grew up on vast farmlands owned by her father in Sorrento, Italy. My grandfather was hired by her father, my great-grandfather, to work on the farm. Years later, he would talk about how lovely Grandma Josephine was in her youth, with long black hair flowing down her back. He quickly fell in love with her. They married, came to the United States, and raised nine children.

My grandfather, also named Luigi, as was my maternal grandfather, would talk of the lush chestnut trees on my great-grandfather's property. It is no wonder, then, why chestnuts were a favorite food in my grandparents' home, perhaps a pleasant reminder of their youthful days when they first met and fell in love. My father tells of a memory, when his father would  come home from a long day of work late at night, after the whole house was sleeping. Grandma Josephine would have a bowl of warm chestnuts ready for my grandfather, and my father would hear him cracking them, one by one.

I usually serve chestnuts at the holidays, and whenever I do,

I think of my father as a little boy, all snug in the warm security of his bed, listening to the sound of my grandparents enjoying those chestnuts. With some attention, it is very easy to roast chestnuts at home.

Roasted Chestnuts

1 pound chestnuts

Cut a clear X on the flat side of each chestnut so that it cuts all the way through the skin. Layer the chestnuts on a baking sheet, and roast at 400°F for forty minutes. Allow to settle for ten minutes, and peel away the skins. Serve with other nuts and fruit.

Camille's Tip: Never allow chestnuts to cool completely before peeling. Once they are fully cooled, peeling will prove difficult.

Uncle Dominick and My Father

My childhood was filled with stories about my uncle Dominick, whom I never had the good fortune of knowing. Uncle Dominick was my father's brother, and the oldest son of nine children: four brothers and five sisters. Although he died as a very young man in World War II, the stories of his life are numerous. I can still recall my aunts and uncles sitting around the table and fondly reminiscing about their cherished oldest brother. My father, especially, who was the seventh child, would tell us of Uncle Dominick's colorful personality, leadership, and dedication to all those he loved.

Uncle Dominick was a genius, an inventor, a prime athlete, a jack-of-all-trades, and a true Renaissance man. He was so brilliant in his academics that his school principal promoted him up two grades, and he scored a 99 percent on the United States Postal Service test. He was a certified lifeguard with an outstanding speed to his stroke. As a teenager, Uncle Dominick started a printing press business in the basement of my grandparents' Brooklyn home, and he continued to engage in successful entrepreneurial adventures until he entered the army.

To my delight, it is reported that Uncle Dominick was also a very talented cook and baker. When anyone would ask my dad about Uncle Dominick's culinary talent and what he would cook, my father's reply was, "Anything! He could make water taste like ice cream!"

According to my father, it was Uncle Dominick's brilliance that allowed him to create his own recipes, especially in his baking. He treated it like a science, and my father would tell us how Uncle Dominick would say, "A good pie is very high."

My father was the last person to see Uncle Dominick in our family. It was World War II, and they were both stationed in California. My father was in Southern California, and Uncle Dominick was at the very northern tip of the state. My father traveled four hundred miles by train to see his brother, as they expected not to see each other for a long time. Uncle Dominick's regiment was being sent overseas.

My father recalls how they went to a movie called *Step Lively* starring Frank Sinatra, and Uncle Dominick predicted that Sinatra would go on to be the greatest entertainer of their entire generation. After the movie, they went to dinner, and Uncle Dominick told my father his vision for their future. He said that he, my dad, and their two other brothers, my uncles Charlie and Danny, were going to team together and open a bakery and restaurant when they all returned home from the war. Together they would work to create the most famous food establishment that New York City would ever see. He was already working on having his food concepts and recipes sent to the patent office in Washington, DC.

That was the final conversation and time my father shared with his oldest brother. At the end of the day, they parted not realizing that it was their last good-bye. A few months later, word was received that Uncle Dominick had been killed overseas. The chaplain of his regiment, Father Robert J. Hearn, wrote Grandma Josephine the following words:

I came in frequent contact with your son, and I can assure you that he was an excellent soldier, esteemed by all and serving his country with honor; but more than this, I can tell you that Dominick served his God loyally and faithfully. He never missed Mass and received Holy Communion at least once a week, so he was fully prepared to meet his God.

In the following decades after World War II, my father and his remaining siblings all continued on to marry, raise families, and be an important and productive part of the Greatest Generation. My father and his brothers did not pursue Uncle Dominick's dream of opening a food establishment, but they all did uphold his legacy in their own small ways. Following Uncle Dominick's lead, my father learned to bake pies for his family, and he always shared his love of baking with me. In remembrance of Uncle Dominick, apple pie was a favorite dessert in our home, and of course, it always had to be very high.

High Apple Pie

8 Golden Delicious apples, peeled, cored, and cut into 1/8-inch slices

1 tablespoon fresh-squeezed lemon juice

3 tablespoons cornstarch

1 cup sugar

1/4 cup light brown sugar

1 teaspoon ground cinnamon

1/8 teaspoon freshly grated nutmeg

2 tablespoons cold unsalted butter, cut into small pieces

1 egg yolk

1 tablespoon milk

In a bowl, toss the apples with lemon juice, cornstarch, white sugar, brown sugar, cinnamon, and nutmeg. Place apples in a single layer on a baking sheet and bake at 350°F for ten minutes. Roll out piecrust dough on a floured work surface and fit it into the pie plate. Layer half the apples into the crust, and dot with half of the butter. Layer the remaining apples into the pie. Dot the remaining butter on top. Roll out the remaining piecrust dough and place carefully over the apples. Pinch the edges to seal the crusts together. Cut slits in the top crust. Mix the egg yolk and milk and brush the top crust. Sprinkle with additional sugar. Bake for one hour in preheated oven at 350°F. Cool at least two hours on a wire rack before serving.

Camille's Tip: Halfway through baking time, cover the edges of the crust with aluminum foil to prevent overbrowning.

Piecrust

2 cups, plus 2 tablespoons flour, plus extra for rolling

1 teaspoon salt

1/3 cup very cold vegetable shortening, cut into pieces

1/2 cup very cold butter, cut into pieces

4 to 6 tablespoons ice water

In a bowl, stir together the flour and salt. Cut in vegetable shortening and butter with a pastry cutter until small lumps form. Sprinkle in water, one tablespoon at a time, tossing with fork until all flour is moistened and pastry dough almost cleans side of bowl. Add an additional teaspoon or two of ice water if necessary. The ingredients should not bind together completely. On a floured work surface, form pastry dough into two separate balls and flatten out the shape. With a floured rolling pin, roll pastry two inches larger than the pie plate.

Camille's Tip: When making a piecrust from scratch, always use cold ingredients. I also take my tools, the bowl, and my pastry cutter and chill them as well. The ideal is for everything to be ice-cold.

A Cup of Cappuccino with Father John

When my niece, Christina, was born in 1984, we were told that she had a mysterious infection of which the origins were unknown. As she had to spend some time in intensive care, we were terribly worried and prayed for a good outcome.

It was during this time that we met a visiting priest to our parish. His name was Father John, and he was from Uganda. Father John accompanied my sister and brother-in-law to see Christina at the hospital, and he prayed with our family. Eventually, within a few days, the infection cleared, all the tests results were negative of any serious illness, and my niece was sent home to begin a healthy and happy life.

The bonus for our family was that we now had a new friend in Father John. My parents invited him to our home on more than one occasion. We had wonderful times with Father John as he spoke to us about his life's path in serving God and our brothers and sisters in Christ. I was amazed at his unselfishness and spirituality.

When he would have dinner with us, Father John was happy to taste our cooking, and he especially enjoyed Italian espresso and cappuccino brewed from rich roasted coffee beans. He loved foods from different cultures and told us that he wished to go back to Uganda and teach the young people about the Italian food and coffee he tasted in our home. He intended to show them how to make pizza and cappuccino. He talked further about how much work there was to be done in his country. He told us of the turmoil in Uganda that involved high levels of illness, as well as the banditry raging back to the seventies that had led to many orphans and a great deal of poverty. It was Father John's great wish to make a significant difference in his country and change the climate of poverty and illness for coming generations. He especially wished to help young women feel empowered and reach their very highest potential.

I initially kept in touch with Father John, but eventually we lost contact. He was at the Vatican at one point and traveling all over the world for the Catholic Church. As life went on and I married, had children, and then divorced, I had cause to seek out Father John and his gentle prayers. I especially needed to reconnect when I found my middle son with autism and my oldest son with cancer. In all that time, I was never able to find him again.

Years later, I became friends with a Ugandan woman, named Robinah, who I met in a prayer group. Robinah was familiar with Father John and his ministry. She promised to help connect us once again. Sometime later, I received an e-mail from her, advising me to call a certain Catholic church in New England because Father John was visiting there for a space of time. I called immediately, but I had just missed him. I asked the woman working at the rectory if she could please pass a message to him and give him my phone number.

Time went by, and I almost forgot how I came so close to communicating with Father John once again, until one evening. My cell phone rang.

The voice on the other end said, "Hello, Camille, this is Father John from Uganda."

I had not heard his voice in over twenty-five years. I immediately started to cry. My son had passed away just a few years earlier, and I did not know which traumatic event to tell this priest of first. I talked so fast and told him of my middle son's autism and my oldest son's cancer. He was terribly sorry for everything, and before we talked further, he wanted to stop and pray. We prayed, deeply, with hope and inspiration. Then he told me of all he had been doing in the past twenty-five years since we last had seen each other.

After Father John left the United States, he went on to become the founder of a charitable organization that provides food, clothing, shelter, and education for more than five thousand children in Uganda. Later on, he built a hospital that is run by doctors, and some of them had received funding for their education when they were children under Father John's guidance.

Father John Bashobora is now very well known in South Africa as a strong evangelizing priest who cares for those who are facing dire difficulties. He travels to many other African nations to encourage others to do the same.

When he returned to Africa after his time in the United States, he carried the memory of the food he tasted in my mother's home, and he shared those thoughts with the young people. My mother was so very thrilled that her small part of what she does was a part of something so significant and meaningful in another part of the world via Father John and his outstanding life's work.

 Inspired by Father John's love of cappuccino, it is my pleasure to share the simple and short technique. It is very easy to prepare this Italian coffee drink in your home even if you do not own a costly espresso machine, which can run into hundreds of dollars. Follow the easy steps, and you will enjoy an aromatic cappuccino with your favorite dessert in no time, just as Father John did in our home.

Cappuccino

Fresh-brewed espresso coffee

1 cup cold milk

Cinnamon or nutmeg

Sugar

Brew a strong pot of espresso in an oven-top espresso pot. In a saucepan, over medium heat, continually beat the milk with a wire whisk. Bubbles will appear and a froth will be created as whisking continues. Do not allow the milk to boil. Remove saucepan from heat, and continue to whisk until the froth is about fifty percent greater in size. Allow the froth to settle for about thirty seconds so the steamed milk is at the bottom of the saucepan and the froth at the top. Pour the steamed milk into the cappuccino cups and then spoon the frothy and foamy milk on top. Pour the espresso down the inside edge of the mug. Sprinkle cinnamon or nutmeg on top.

Alice Campbell and Her Pot Roast

Alice and Dave Campbell were my parents' lifelong friends and their dear neighbors for many decades. Alice, like my mom, was a stay-at-home mom, and Dave was a detective for the New York City Police Department. Together, Alice and Dave raised four children, David, Jamie, Johnny, and Alice. Along with other families on our block, we all grew up together in the Bay Ridge section of Brooklyn, and it was a very happy childhood and family life for one and all.

Alice had an engaging and creative personality. She was the neighborhood mom who taught us how to sing Christmas carols and dive in the pool during summertime. She put together a club for all the little girls on our block called "The Fancy Friday Girls." Every Friday, we would gather in Alice's home, and she would teach us to knit, crochet, and bake. Her home was a busy one, and her door was always open. She had a custom-built kitchen in her finished basement, and it was there that she held court, always inviting one and all for a visit, a cup of coffee, or a large meal.

While I was writing this book, her daughter, also named Alice, reminisced with me. "She loved to cook, and on any given day, she would be cooking for more than just the six of us, because one or all of us kids would have at least one friend over almost every night for dinner. I recall, in the summers, she would be cooking for sometimes up to fifteen people!"

Other than Alice's joy of life, it was the memory of her

strength in the face of adversity that I took with me into my own adulthood. Her third son, Johnny, was born with Down syndrome. Being the parent of a special child is a path that one never expects to walk when planning a family. When I was faced with the path ahead of my Nicky's diagnosis of autism, I often thought of Alice and her refusal to be defeated in the face of Johnny's Down syndrome. Alice met the challenge and stayed resilient, always keeping her uplifting energy while she went about her day raising her family. She set an example, cooked up a storm, and ultimately loved the life that she had with her husband, children, family, and friends.

Her daughter, Alice, and her son David shared their mother's recipe for pot roast. I was especially happy to have the pot roast recipe because one night, many years ago, when my parents were at one of Alice's dinner parties, she prepared her pot roast. In the following years, my father always told everyone that Alice Campbell made the best pot roast he had ever tasted!

Pot Roast

Eye of round roast, 3 to 4 pounds

Table salt and black pepper, to taste

1 stick of sweet butter

3 cups beef stock

2 tablespoons flour

2 teaspoons Gravy Master

Salt and pepper all sides of roast. In a large pot, melt butter. Brown all sides of eye of round in order to create a nice sear. Add beef stock. Cook on low heat for three to four hours. Remove meat from pot and allow settling.

Whisk flour and beef stock into meat drippings until a medium consistency is reached. Add Gravy Master, stirring continuously, until gravy is thick. Serve eye of round and gravy with mashed potatoes and vegetables.

Auntie Sally's Shrimps

Auntie Sally, who lived across the street from Alice Campbell, was an aunt to one of my oldest and most cherished friends, Sandra. When we were ten years old, Sandra's mother passed from breast cancer. Sandra's dad, Dimitri, continued on as a very fine single parent to his five children. However, when it came to the cooking, it was Auntie Sally who took the reins.

Auntie Sally was born on Rhode Island and came to New York with her family at a very young age. As the oldest, she cared for her younger siblings and learned to cook. Her father discouraged her from marrying because he wanted her to continue to care for the family. Auntie Sally became an operator in the New York City garment industry and remained dedicated to her family in every chapter of her life.

By the time I knew Auntie Sally, she was a charming middle-aged woman who was wildly and bluntly talkative and known as the mayor of her block. She was always excitable and always happy, while at the same time innocently critical. I really cannot recall her ever being in a poor mood. She would lovingly scold her many nieces and nephews while she cooked meal after splendid meal in her kitchen. Almost every time I entered Auntie Sally's home, she was cooking, with her apron firmly in place. As Auntie Sally was Arabic American, I found her food very fascinating.

Auntie Sally's interest in cooking and food never dimmed, and she always had a packed house as she served her many visitors. She loved to watch Julia Child and *The Galloping Gourmet* on TV. As she grew older and entered her senior years, she was an avid cook for the Syrian Orthodox Church and their many events. Even when she finally entered a nursing home, she taught the staff how to prepare authentic Arabic food in the kitchen.

When Sandra and I spoke about Auntie Sally's most memorable recipe, we realized the one that stands out is not even of Arabic origin. Auntie Sally is remembered for her excellent shrimp curry, which she always liked to serve with a mango chutney. To this day, Auntie Sally's nieces and nephews still prepare this dish while remembering her festive and happy spirit from years gone by.

Shrimp Curry

1/2 cup extra-virgin olive oil

4 garlic cloves, peeled and crushed

1 tablespoon curry powder

1 cup fresh flat-leaf parsley, chopped

8 plum tomatoes, chopped

1 pound jumbo shrimp

Kosher salt and freshly ground black pepper

Half of a fresh-squeezed lemon (optional)

2 cups cooked rice

In a large pot, warm olive oil over medium heat. Combine garlic, curry, and parsley and cook for five minutes. Follow with tomatoes and simmer for forty-five minutes. Mix in shrimp and cook until pink, about five minutes. Add salt and pepper. Stir in fresh lemon juice and stir well. Serve over white rice with mango chutney on the side.

Mango Chutney

3 cups half-ripe mangoes, peeled and chopped

1 cup brown sugar

1 cup cider vinegar

1/2 cup golden raisins

2 teaspoons fresh ginger, peeled and grated

2 garlic cloves, peeled and minced

1 teaspoon cayenne pepper

Kosher salt

In a large sauté pan, over medium heat, combine all ingredients and bring to a boil. Reduce heat to low and simmer, uncovered, for one hour and until thick. Stir occasionally. Allow chutney to cool, and keep refrigerated in jars.

My Young Cooking Students

In this life, a privileged few come across a career opportunity that cannot be measured. I am glad to say I am one of those fortunate people. I took on a project that continually left me in awe and filled with inspiration when I became part of a broad-reaching private school that caters to learning-challenged students starting at the elementary level and on to high school. It was here that I developed a culinary program that enabled me to instruct the fine art of cooking to students who had an enthusiasm for the world of food.

Equipped with a stocked kitchen, I set out to teach the students the joys of cooking. Our program became an important part of the school community, and one and all enjoyed the culinary delights the students were taught to prepare.

The smaller children, in the elementary grades, were just as enthusiastic as the older ones and knew me as "Camille, the lady that likes to cook." One day, a little boy named Dillon asked me if I would like to have one of "his" recipes. Dillon was only eight years old, and I was charmed by his offer. I told him, yes, of course, I would love to hear his recipe. He recited a recipe for pomegranates, mango, and honeydew tossed with a warmed glaze of juice and cider. Later on, I spoke to Dillon's mother and told her of my conversation with her son. She was pleased that he had recited the recipe and told me that it was actually one they prepared in their home

In Dillon's class was a little boy named Julian. During the Jewish holidays, Julian would happily tell the classroom of the many traditions his family enjoyed, food included. He would share favorite family songs that were played to celebrate Hanukkah, and he would tell us of the potato latkes that were enjoyed by all in his home. For Passover, a festival that commemorates the story of the Exodus when the ancient Israelites were freed from slavery in Egypt, Julian's family would enjoy fish balls. I completely enjoyed Julian's passionate and informative recital each time, and I also enjoyed talking to his parents about their food preparations for their special events and holidays. To my delight, Julian's dad, Adrian, shared his recipe for Moroccan fish balls with me.

Then there was Patrick, also an eight-year-old and a budding gourmet. He had a passion for food and loved to be involved with my teachings at the school. I instantly knew Patrick came from a home where fine ingredients and good cooking were strong values. I could tell by the creative lunches that Patrick would bring to school, which included fresh rolls filled with French cheeses and meats, hummus with pita chips, and fresh sushi.

Upon communicating with Patrick's mom, Susan, she informed me that he had helped her cook since he was two years old. They started with scrambled eggs and cheese omelets, pancakes, cakes, and cookies. When Patrick was seven, Susan graduated him to other food experiences: meatballs, guacamole, and homemade pizza. He even kneaded his own dough. Eventually, Patrick was nearly able to make these simple but tasty foods by himself, and almost from memory. Susan would send us pictures of him baking the fresh pizza topped with gourmet ingredients. Those pictures would truly make my day, and I was very happy when Susan shared a terrific turkey meatball recipe that Patrick made so very well.

One early afternoon, I prepared mozzarella en carozza. Patrick enjoyed this immensely, and from that time on, when he would ask me when I would be

making "mozzarella en carozza," he would pronounce it in an Italian accent. Of course, now whenever I prepare that particular dish, I can hear little Patrick's excited voice pronouncing the words in that fashion.

Among my older students, there was a teen named Dionysis. He had an engaging smile, and on the very first day of cooking class he arrived wearing his own chef jacket with his name embroidered on the breast pocket. Dionysis was a cooking instructor's dream student. He had a passion for food and a joy of cooking. He also had an amazing ability to lead the rest of the class with his enthusiasm toward learning and tasting the next food adventure in my kitchen-classroom.

Many of the passions of food and cooking begin for us as youngsters. Almost every person you will ever talk to who has a career in food, or simply a great love of preparing food, will tell you how the seeds were planted in their early youth. I was thrilled to have the opportunity to "plant" a few seeds at this special school. I look forward to the years ahead when I may see the final bloom.

Dillon's Pomegranates

1 cup pomegranate seeds

2 mangoes, peeled and sliced

1 honeydew, peeled and sliced

1 cup pomegranate juice

1 cup apple cider

3/4 cup sugar

Mix the fruits in a bowl. In a saucepan, warm pomegranate juice, apple cider, and sugar. Bring to a boil, and then simmer until thickened. Pour over fruits, and serve with vanilla ice cream!

Julian and Adrian's Moroccan Fish Balls

1 pound ground whiting fish

1/2 cup matzo meal

Kosher salt and freshly ground black pepper

1 teaspoon, plus 1 tablespoon cumin

3 tablespoons olive oil

3 garlic cloves, peeled and sliced

1 28-ounce can crushed tomatoes

1 tablespoon paprika

1 hot chili pepper

1/4 cup fresh flat-leaf parsley

1/4 cup chicken stock

1 cup water

In a bowl, mix the whiting, matzo meal, salt, pepper, one teaspoon cumin, and one tablespoon of the olive oil. Chill overnight.

Form the chilled whiting fish into balls and set aside. In a saucepot, warm remaining olive oil over medium heat. Add garlic, and cook until tender. Add tomatoes, remaining cumin, paprika, hot chili pepper, parsley, chicken stock, water, salt, and pepper. Reduce heat to low, and simmer for thirty minutes. Remove the chili pepper. Add the fish balls to the pot of sauce, and simmer an additional thirty minutes.

Camille's Tip: Adrian advises us to remove the chili pepper thirty minutes into the cooking process. However, if you greatly enjoy the heat of chili peppers, then you may keep it in there the whole time. If you do not enjoy a lot of heat, then you may remove the chili pepper even earlier than the suggested thirty minutes.

Mozzarella en Carozza

4 slices of fresh white bread, crusts removed

2 slices fresh mozzarella, 1/3-inch thick

2 slices of prosciutto

4 leafs fresh basil

2 eggs

2 tablespoons heavy cream

1/2 cup flour

Vegetable oil for frying

Parmigiano-Reggiano cheese, grated

Lemon slices

Marinara Sauce (page 227)

Place two slices of white bread on a clean work surface. Place a slice of mozzarella on each slice of bread, and then repeat with a slice of prosciutto. Top with two pieces of basil each. Cover with remaining two pieces of white bread to create a sandwich. Beat eggs very well and mix with heavy cream. Carefully dip each sandwich in the eggs and then the flour. In a sauté pan, warm vegetable oil over medium heat. Fry the sandwiches on each side until golden brown. Allow to settle for two minutes and then cut diagonally across. Sprinkle with Parmigiano-Reggiano, and garnish with lemon slices. Serve with marinara sauce.

Patrick's Turkey Meatballs

1 egg

1$^1/_3$ pounds ground turkey

3/4 cup unseasoned bread crumbs

2 garlic cloves

1 shallot, chopped fine

1/2 small pepper (red, yellow, or orange), chopped fine

1 tablespoon Greek oregano

1$^1/_2$ tablespoons of small nonpareil capers or alcaparrado olive mix

1$^1/_2$ tablespoons flat-leaf parsley, chopped

1/8 teaspoon crushed red pepper flakes, or to taste

Kosher salt, or sea salt, and freshly ground black pepper

Olive oil

In a medium bowl, beat egg well. Add ground turkey and bread crumbs and mix with hands. Place garlic into a garlic presser and add to mixture. Add shallot, peppers, Greek oregano, capers or alcaparrado, parsley, red pepper flakes, salt, and pepper. Form into small balls.

In a sauté pan, warm a small amount of olive oil over medium-high heat. Brown the meatballs, turning them continually in order to brown all sides well. Finish cooking them for at least ten minutes in the red sauce of your choice.

Camille's Tip: Susan advised not to use the breast of the turkey for this recipe, as it is too dry.

Lucy and Her Rice Pudding

It is often said that one must love to cook in order to be a good cook. However, I do firmly believe that any person who does not particularly enjoy time in the kitchen can still offer enjoyable edibles to please their family and friends. One can also signal that a lot of love was put into the preparation of the dish. This pretty much sums up the cooking scenario when it comes to my sister, Lucy.

In our family, Lucy is the serious business mind, and I am the creative wild child. While we are known as a perfect pair for hosting large formal parties and charity functions, we each support a different side to the project. Lucy handles the finances and the organizational tasks, and I breathe excitement into the theme of the event. Suffice it to say, it is always quite a ride for everyone involved.

My sister will often tell people how she prefers not to step into the kitchen. A restaurateur for over thirty years, she has an adoration and educated knowledge of fine food, but she would rather have somebody else do the cooking as opposed to herself.

In spite of my sister's lack of culinary enthusiasm, she has mastered more than one dish and especially one in particular. Lucy makes the best rice pudding I have ever tasted. The recipe was given to her by a long ago colleague named Nellie Rothstein. My sister was so taken with the rich creamy taste that boasted such pure ingredients, that she was determined to make it her signature dessert in all the following years.

Lucy did master that pudding, and as the years went by it was greatly anticipated by our family and friends for our many gatherings. I still recall a Thanksgiving project that my son, Christopher, did for his teacher when he was a little boy. He was asked to list all the things he was grateful for during the holiday season of giving thanks. He listed his family, friends, toys, and games. The very last item on the list was "and Aunt Lucy's rice pudding!"

Rice Pudding

1 cup Carolina rice

2 cups cold water

2 quarts and 1 cup milk

1 cup sugar

2 eggs, beaten

1/2 teaspoon vanilla

1/2 teaspoon cinnamon

1/2 teaspoon nutmeg

In a large pot, bring rice, water, 2 quarts of milk and sugar to a full boil. Lower to a simmer for forty five minutes while stirring constantly. Rice should be soft. Stir in eggs, remaining milk, vanilla, cinnamon and nutmeg. Bring to a complete boil. Lower to a simmer for five minutes while stirring constantly. Remove immediately from heat and pour pudding into a deep casserole dish. Sprinkle a bit more cinnamon on top. Cool completely and refrigerate. Serve cold.

Camille's tip: It is best to make this recipe the day before as the pudding will settle into a desired and creamy firmness.

Joan Lane and Her Irish Soda Bread

I have always been a lover of Irish soda bread, and of course, I had the desire to bake it myself rather than purchase it from our local bakery. For a long time, I was on a quest to find the very best recipe possible. Upon exploration, I found that not every Irish family has the same recipe, but eventually I did find an exceptional one, and it came from my sons' second-grade teacher, Joan Lane.

Before retiring after a long and fruitful career, Joan taught second grade at our local elementary school. When my sons Frankie and Christopher each entered her class, I was fully aware that they were about to benefit from a master who simply had the art of teaching down to a science.

However, "Mrs. Lane" was a tough-love teacher. She was strict and did not tolerate nonsense. My sons, although bright and basically good boys, did have their moments of boundless energy. In later years, I owed their fine grammar and strong reading skills to Joan, who, until this day, I am glad to call a friend.

During my feverish desire to uncover the best Irish soda bread recipe on the planet, Joan, and her daughter Mary Ann were happy to present their recipe, which had a story of its own.

Joan and her husband, Bill, were friends with the Hayden family. Mary Ann told me that the "Hayden Irish soda bread" was the very best recipe she had ever encountered and the taste was incomparable. Mary Ann would bake this recipe for many coworkers, and she was soon known for her Irish soda bread at her workplace and everywhere else that she shared it with others. One day, a new woman joined her staff, and she also baked Irish soda bread that was remarkably scrumptious like Mary Ann's. Upon talking to the woman, Mary Ann found that this woman's family was also friends with the Hayden Family, and she was also baking their recipe!

However, before finally sharing their recipe, years ago, the Hayden family was very secretive on the best way to bake Irish soda bread. Bill Lane cajoled, pleaded, and asked for years, but the Hayden Family refused to reveal the delicious details to him.

Decades passed by, and one evening, Joan and Bill were in the company of Mrs. Hayden. Bill was determined to finally get that recipe. He spent the evening helping Mrs. Hayden enjoy quite a few drinks. Happily imbibed, Mrs. Hayden, under Bill's guidance, finally and graciously gave him the recipe.

I baked this soda bread many times in my kitchen, and each time I was not disappointed. In fact, I was quite elated! The crust comes out to a deep golden hue. The warm inside of the loaf is buttery, with the moist flavor of rich raisins and caraway seeds. My thanks to the Lane family, and also the Hayden family.

Irish Soda Bread

4 cups flour

1/2 teaspoon salt

4 teaspoons baking powder

1/2 cup sugar

2 tablespoons vegetable shortening

1 cup raisins

1 cup currants

2 tablespoons caraway seeds

2 eggs

1 cup milk

In a bowl, stir together the flour, salt, baking powder, and sugar. Cut in vegetable shortening with a pastry cutter. Rinse raisins and currants with water. Shake a little flour over them. Add them, along with the caraway seeds, to dry mixture. Beat eggs. Add milk to eggs, and then slowly add to dry mixture. Mix well and form into dough. Place dough in a round glass baking dish or standard loaf pan. Bake in a preheated oven at 350°F for fifty minutes.

Chef Pnina Peled

Food can certainly lend an uplifting twist to the process of physical and mental healing. The spirit, work, and life of my friend Chef Pnina Peled is a testament to this fact. I first met her when she made a major career change into the world of the childhood cancer community.

Pnina was born in Israel, and grew up in Brooklyn, helping out her father, who was the owner of more than one food establishment. Realizing her love for working with food, she attended culinary school and went on to become a high-end chef in the best restaurants and hotels in New York City. She made appearances with Rachael Ray, and also on the Food Network, where she was a winner on the popular show *Chopped*.

Clearly such accomplishments were pivotal high points for any chef. But for Pnina, there was much more to her purpose and a greater reason for her talent. She answered a very noble calling by becoming executive chef at one of the highest-profile hospitals in the world, Memorial Sloan-Kettering Cancer Center. Pnina was compelled toward this opportunity because she hoped to make a bigger impact with cooking where it was most needed.

At Memorial Sloan-Kettering, Pnina led the way as a pioneer. Cancer patients often have to deal with a low-sodium, low-sugar, and low-microbial diet. The result is that patients do not eat as well as they should, and they rarely enjoy a good meal.

Pnina was determined to change that scenario, and she did,

with much success. She transformed poor and often tasteless hospital food into a broad and exciting menu of food choices. She began by spending a great amount of time by the bedsides of the patients, with a specific concentration on the children. Pnina learned about the children and their likes and dislikes in food. She put her creativity to work with recipes that stayed within the dietary guidelines, but allowed them to eat enjoyable and tasty dishes once again. Pnina would even make fresh-baked pizza and present it to the children in a pizza box so that they would have the feel of a special pizza delivery right to their hospital room.

For Pnina, the most satisfying part of her job is when a child who has been having eating difficulties finally eats and truly enjoys that meal. Having a relationship with the children through food has become one of her greatest professional accomplishments.

Pnina's work in using food to enrich the lives of child cancer patients is a tremendous foodship, and it simply leaves me in

awe. As a mom from the childhood cancer world, and as a dedicated cook who is constantly romanced by the connections, emotions, and love that food brings into our lives, it is my great pleasure to share a recipe that Pnina very generously gave me to include in this book, for orange panna cotta. Thank you, Pnina. This world is better, and definitely more delicious, because of you.

Orange Panna Cotta

5 pieces gelatin

3 cups cream

1 cup milk

5 ounces sugar

8 ounces orange concentrate

Zest of one orange, finely grated

1 vanilla bean

Place the gelatin in cold water. In a medium pot, mix cream, milk, sugar, orange concentrate, orange zest, and the vanilla bean. Bring to a boil. Boil for at least five minutes on low heat. Take out the vanilla bean, and add the gelatin. Mix well and evenly divide into eight ramekins. Place into a storage container and cool to room temperature before refrigerating. Refrigerate for at least two hours before serving.

The Two Toms

In this world, there are some people who are so exuberantly unique that knowing them is an experience.

Thomas Roggeman and Tom Kane were my cherished friends who I met almost simultaneously. Although the two never met, they each were the personification of good in their own way. They were what I refer to as human sunshine, spreaders of what God wants in this world and in this life. They both had huge personalities, gentle hearts, and they never saw any bad in others, or at least, they were each too much of a gentleman to mention any bad they saw.

Thomas Roggeman, also known as Rock to all those who knew and loved him, stepped into my life when I needed to remain true to my faith and understand that life must go on even after losing a child. He was a graduate of the University of Notre Dame, where he played football as linebacker and nose guard. His career path was that of a very dedicated college football coach, first at Alabama State and then East Carolina University. He coached defensive tackles and took a deep interest in the moral and spiritual path of his players. His passionate words were, "Over the years, I have had players come up to me for just about any problem that you can imagine. As a coach, you pray that these young men listen to you and live life the correct way."

Rock and I spent many happy times in deep conversation. We often spoke of his Polish roots, his love of dancing, and his dedication to his family. I especially enjoyed hearing about his love for Polish cuisine and his favorite desserts.

Knowing I was an avid cook, he excitedly asked me, "Please tell me that you bake German chocolate cake!" The bad news was that I had never baked a German chocolate cake. However, encouraged by Rock's enthusiasm, I was interested in mastering the dessert, and eventually I did. A foodship was created.

Tom Kane was a journalist, a gentle giant of a man, and the ultimate people person. He ran his own community theater and took a great interest in developing fresh talent and helping young people on their path in the creative arts. His love of the stage, whether acting, producing, or directing, touched all those who knew him well. He recognized, without prejudice, the best in everyone and in everything, whether a sporting event, play, book, or song. Tom saw everyone's potential, whether he knew them professionally or personally, and he loved to hear each person's story.

At the very end of Tom's life, I spent an afternoon at his bedside. It was the last time I ever saw him, and it was our final long talk. He told me that he had lived a life of so many happy days that they could not be counted. He also told me that he did not want to leave this life because he loved it and it was worth fighting for. However, he said that he had faith in Christ.

He said that people, knowing he was a journalist, would come up to him and whisper, "I do a little writing myself."

Tom would happily respond, "Why are you whispering about it? Shout it out!"

As I sat there holding his hand, it came to me that I had no idea what Tom's favorite food was, and I wanted to have that knowledge in the coming years when I held comforting thoughts of him. And so I said, "Do you realize that with all the talking you and I have done over the years about our favorite restaurants that you have never told me your favorite food?"

He replied, "That's because I have so many!"

And Tom, a man who died a few days later, let out a booming laugh over thoughts of his favorite culinary pleasures.

Then he said, "Well, let me tell you about a favorite childhood memory. When I was a little boy, my grandmother worked in a German deli, and she made the best potato pancakes I ever tasted!"

When Tom told me this, I made a special note in my mind that I would learn to make German potato pancakes in tribute to Tom and his grandmother.

Both Toms passed away within six months of each other. Even when diagnosed with cancer, both men, not even for an instant, allowed the illness to dim their engaging spirits.

Now, as I prepare German chocolate cake and German potato pancakes, I recall the smile on the faces of the two Toms and their love of life and people.

German Chocolate Cake

4 ounces of sweetened Baker's chocolate

2 cups flour

1 cup cocoa powder

$1^1/_2$ teaspoon baking powder

$1^1/_2$ teaspoon baking soda

1/2 teaspoon salt

1 cup coffee

1 cup buttermilk

1 cup oil

$1^1/_2$ cups sugar

3 eggs

1 teaspoon vanilla

Chop the chocolate into small pieces and melt over a double boiler. In a bowl, sift the flour, cocoa powder, baking powder, baking soda, and salt. Set aside. In a small bowl, combine the coffee and buttermilk. In the bowl of an electric mixer, or with a hand mixer, beat the oil and the sugar, and add the eggs, one at a time. Add the vanilla extract. Combine all three mixtures and beat until ingredients are well blended. Fold in the melted chocolate.

Divide the batter evenly among two round greased pans. Bake in a preheated oven at 375°F for thirty to thirty-five minutes. Remove from oven, and allow to cool in pan for 20 minutes. Remove cakes and transfer to wire racks to cool further. After cakes are completely cooled, apply the frosting.

Frosting:

1 cup evaporated milk

1 ¼ cup sugar

3 egg yolks, beaten

1/2 cup butter

1 teaspoon vanilla

1 cup coconut flakes

1 ¼ cup toasted pecans, coarsely chopped

In a medium saucepan, cook the evaporated milk, sugar, egg yolks, and butter over medium heat. Stir constantly until the mixture begins to boil and thicken. Remove from heat, and stir in the pecans, coconut, and vanilla extract. Allow to cool. Do not frost the sides of the cake, but rather frost in between the layers and on top.

German Potato Pancakes

2 large eggs

1/4 cup flour

1 teaspoon baking powder

Kosher salt and freshly ground black pepper

5 russet potatoes, peeled and finely shredded

1 small onion, diced

Butter

Sour cream

In a large bowl, beat together eggs, flour, baking powder, salt, and pepper. Mix in potatoes and onion. Warm butter, starting with one tablespoon, on a griddle or sauté pan, over medium heat. With a quarter-cup measuring cup, pour the batter for each pancake and cook on each side until golden. Serve with a dollop of sour cream.

Part Three
Taste

"I don't like gourmet cooking or this cooking or that cooking.
I like good cooking."~James Beard

The following pages are some of the recipes from my own repertoire. Yes, just some, because I do have many more! Many of the recipes in part three are my originals and others are recipes that were taught to me and that I re-developed to make my own. I have been cooking since my childhood, and I began in a professional environment at the age of sixteen. By the time I was a young mother, I partnered in a first restaurant and soon after became a caterer. Engaging in cooking demonstrations and food writing allowed me to broaden my canvas even wider. Spending years cooking with others in the New York City metro area allowed me to satisfy my curiosity in learning more culinary delights. Eventually I moved on as a cooking instructor to learning-challenged children. Finally, and with a true sense of accomplishment, I now sit down to share my knowledge. Pouring out my culinary experiences from my kitchen to yours is a privilege.

Breakfast

In this day and age, breakfast is too often just a necessary task when we are in a hurry to begin a busy day and need to pop a morsel of quick nutrition into our mouths. However, in my mind, this makes

breakfast on a day off, and especially the weekends and holiday mornings, even more special. One of the most pleasant things life has to offer is a relaxed breakfast on a lazy Sunday morning, or friends coming over for a late Saturday morning gathering to enjoy a breakfast buffet.

Eggs in Bread Buckets

"Love and eggs are best when they are fresh." ~Russian proverb

I am not too sure if I agree about the love part, as our love for each other can grow more and more with each passing year. However, I certainly agree that eggs are best used fresh and especially for the following recipe. I first started to make eggs cooked in bread when I saw a scene in the movie *Moonstruck*, which starred Cher. Her mom, played by Olympia Dukakis, was frying eggs inside a round circle of French bread. I thought that looked very appealing, and so, of course, I tried it. From there, I started to bake eggs in rolls. Cutting into the crusty bread and having the yolk ooze out is a delight!

4 round dinner rolls

2 tablespoons butter, softened

2 garlic cloves, peeled

1/2 cup basil, chopped

4 jumbo large eggs

Kosher salt and freshly ground black pepper

1/8 teaspoon crushed red pepper flakes

4 sun-dried tomatoes, diced

Parmigiano-Reggiano grated cheese

Slice off top of each dinner roll. Carefully remove the inside of the bread to create a hollow, making sure the bottom of the roll remains intact. Spread the softened butter on the inside of each roll. Grate the garlic cloves so that the garlic falls into the hole of each dinner roll. Sprinkle in half the basil. Crack an egg into each dinner roll. Sprinkle salt, pepper, and red pepper flakes. Add a teaspoon of diced sun-dried tomato and sprinkle with the remaining basil. Top with a generous amount of Parmigiano-Reggiano cheese. On a baking sheet, bake in a preheated oven at 350°F for 17 minutes or until bread is toasted golden at the edges.

Camille's Tip: Use eggs and butter that are room temperature, unless a recipe specifically calls for cold.

Morning Risotto

Risotto with breakfast bacon is a great way to start the day on a cold winter morning, when a hearty and hot breakfast is most appreciated. I also prepare this dish with breakfast sausage. When making risotto, constant stirring is the key to success. Prepare to use a lot of elbow action!

3 cups water

1 tablespoon chicken base

4 tablespoons butter

4 slices thick bacon, cut into small pieces

1 shallot, chopped

1 cup Arborio rice

Parmigiano-Reggiano cheese, grated

Kosher salt and freshly ground black pepper

1 tablespoon fresh flat-leaf parsley, chopped

In a pot, boil water and chicken base and then bring down to a simmer very low. In an additional pot, melt half of the butter over medium-high heat. Add bacon and shallots. Sauté until shallots are translucent. Stir in rice, and allow to brown. Continue to stir. Reduce heat, and add half the water and chicken base. Allow rice to slowly absorb the water. Do not stop stirring. Continue with second half of water until fully absorbed. Simmer and stir until risotto is tender and creamy. Take pot off heat, and stir in Parmigiano-

Reggiano cheese, the remaining butter, salt, and pepper. Garnish
with parsley.

Savory Herb French Toast with Red Wine Strawberries

The classic combination of wine, cheese and fruit is not just for an afternoon picnic or a Saturday evening gathering of friends. It can also be part of our morning. Decadent strawberries in red wine is a glorious wake-up for breakfast and goes very well with this French toast that is made with savory flavors as opposed to traditional sweet flavors.

2 cups fresh strawberries, halved

1 cup red wine

1 teaspoon thyme

4 eggs

2 tablespoons heavy cream

1 teaspoon chives, chopped

2 tablespoons Pecorino Romano cheese, grated

Butter

8 slices brioche

In a bowl, mix strawberries, red wine, and thyme, and allow to chill for one hour.

Whisk together the eggs and heavy cream. Stir in the chives and Pecorino Romano. Warm butter, starting with one tablespoon, on a griddle or sauté pan, over medium heat. Dip each brioche in the egg mixture, coating both sides well. Place the brioche, a few at a time, on heat, and cook each side until golden. Serve strawberries with French toast.

French Toast with Raisin Mascarpone

I first started to use mascarpone cheese when preparing tiramisu. Since then, I have found it to be a great addition to so many recipes. The creaminess of the mascarpone, added with refreshing fruits or crunchy nuts, are perfect together.

1 cup raisins, divided

2 tablespoons brandy

$1^3/_4$ cups water

1 cup, plus $1^1/_2$ tablespoons sugar

1/2 cup mascarpone

1 tablespoon heavy cream

8 slices brioche

3 eggs

1 cup milk

Butter

Confectioners' sugar

Soak half the raisins in the brandy overnight. In a small saucepan, heat the raisins and brandy, in their syrup, with the water and one cup of sugar. Bring to a boil and then simmer for twenty minutes. Set raisin syrup aside to cool.

Combine the mascarpone, heavy cream, one and a half tablespoons of the remaining sugar, and the rest of the raisins in a small bowl.

Spread the mascarpone mixture thinly on one slice of brioche, and top with another slice to create a sandwich. Repeat with the remaining slices.

Whisk together the eggs and milk. Warm butter, starting with one tablespoon, on a griddle or sauté pan, over medium heat. Dip each sandwich in the egg mixture, coating sides well. Place the French toast sandwiches, a few at a time, on heat, and cook each side about two minutes or until golden.

Sprinkle a dusting of confectioners' sugar and drizzle raisin syrup over French toast. Serve warm.

Camille's Tip: You can go savory with mascarpone. Just add a splash of olive oil and toss in capers, anchovies, and herbs. Mix well, and you have a great dip for crusty bread or breadsticks.

Eggnog French Toast

This is a delicious addition for a holiday brunch or for breakfast on Christmas morning, after everyone unwraps their presents by the tree. The taste of eggnog in the French toast is just so completely in the holiday spirit!

4 eggs

1/2 cup eggnog

1 teaspoon vanilla

1/2 teaspoon cinnamon

8 slices brioche

Butter

Confectioners' sugar

Whisk together the eggs and eggnog. Stir in vanilla and cinnamon. Warm butter, starting with one tablespoon, on a griddle or sauté pan, over medium heat. Dip each brioche in the egg mixture, coating both sides well. Place the brioche, a few at a time, on heat, and cook each side until golden.

Sprinkle a dusting of confectioners' sugar, and drizzle with a mild-flavored syrup. Serve warm.

Three Berry Pancakes

My youngest son, Christopher, is a big fan of berries. As they are his favorite fruits, very often, I will bring home a variety from the grocer. As he is also a lover of pancakes, I like to add a colorful mix of berries into my pancake batter. When making breakfast for a special loved one, or hosting a breakfast or brunch, there is nothing like a stack of fluffy, buttery, mouthwatering pancakes created from scratch.

1 cup flour

1 teaspoon baking powder

1/2 teaspoon baking soda

1/4 teaspoon salt

1 tablespoon sugar

1 cup milk

1/2 cup sour cream

2 large eggs

1 teaspoon vanilla

2 tablespoons canola oil

1 tablespoon blueberries

1 tablespoon strawberries, sliced

1 tablespoon blackberries

Butter

Confectioners' sugar

In a bowl, sift the flour, baking powder, baking soda, and salt. Add sugar. In a second bowl, whisk milk, sour cream, eggs, vanilla, and oil. Mix dry ingredients with wet ingredients. Add berries. Warm butter, starting with one tablespoon, on a griddle or sauté pan, over medium heat. With a quarter-cup measuring cup, pour the batter for each pancake. Cook on each side until golden, turning when bubbles appear. Add a light dusting of confectioners' sugar, and drizzle with a favorite syrup.

Pumpkin Pancakes

This is a great way to spend an early morning during the autumn season, when our taste buds crave that pumpkin flavor. It is especially a great breakfast selection for Columbus Day weekend.

1 cup flour

1 teaspoon baking powder

1/2 teaspoon baking soda

1/4 teaspoon salt

1 tablespoon sugar

1 teaspoon pumpkin spice

1 cup milk

1/2 cup sour cream

2 tablespoons canned pumpkin puree

2 large eggs

2 tablespoons canola oil

Butter

Confectioners' sugar

In a bowl, sift the flour, baking powder, baking soda, and salt. Add sugar and pumpkin spice. In a second bowl, whisk milk, sour cream, pumpkin puree, eggs, and oil. Mix dry ingredients with wet ingredients. Warm butter, starting with one tablespoon, on a griddle or sauté pan, over medium heat. With a quarter-cup measuring cup, pour the batter for each pancake. Cook on each side until golden,

turning when bubbles appear. Add a light dusting of confectioners'
sugar, and drizzle with a favorite syrup.

Simple Scramblers

"I have had, in my time, memorable meals of scrambled eggs with fresh truffles, scrambled eggs with caviar, and other glamorous things, but to me, there are few things as magnificent as scrambled eggs, pure and simple, perfectly cooked and perfectly seasoned."
~James Beard

I completely agree with James Beard. There is nothing like a simple dish of scrambled eggs, and they will come out fluffy and perfect as long as you stir the eggs constantly and slowly in the pan. On any given morning, my sons are happy to enjoy a few scrambled eggs with a pat of butter, a toasty warm English muffin, and a cool glass of fresh orange juice.

6 large eggs
$1^1/_2$ tablespoons butter
2 tablespoons Parmigiano-Reggiano cheese, grated
Flat-leaf parsley for garnish

In a medium bowl, whisk the eggs until frothy. In a sauté pan, warm butter over medium heat. Turn the heat down to low, and pour the eggs into the sauté pan and allow to set a few moments. Using a spatula, cook the eggs by stirring constantly but slowly toward the center of the pan. Tilt the sauté pan to cook the runny parts as fluffy clouds are created. Remove the eggs from pan while slightly underdone. Top with Parmigiano-Reggiano. Sprinkle with parsley, and serve with English muffins or crusty bread.

Ham and Cheese Breakfast Strata

"Call me all-American, but I love ham-and-cheese sandwiches. And not just any old ham-and-cheese sandwich. My mother's is the best. I've tried many times to make these sandwiches on my own, but it's never the same." ~Andy Roddick

Few of us would disagree with the famous athlete Andy Roddick on the all-American love of ham and cheese. So, of all the ways to prepare strata, I usually take the simple ham-and-cheese route. Strata is very functional if serving it to guests for a breakfast gathering, as you can prepare it and refrigerate it, unbaked, the night before your company arrives.

12 slices hearty white bread

1 cup Swiss cheese, shredded

1 cup ham, diced

2 tablespoons scallions

8 large eggs

2 tablespoons Dijon mustard

1 cup milk

Kosher salt and freshly ground black pepper

Lightly grease a twelve-by-nine baking dish, and arrange half the bread slices in the bottom. Sprinkle with half of the cheese and ham. Arrange a second layer with the remaining slices of bread. Sprinkle the remaining cheese and ham. Beat the scallion, eggs, Dijon mustard, milk, salt, and pepper. Slowly pour over the bread slices, allowing the egg mixture to absorb into the bread well. If necessary, spoon egg mixture over any uncoated bread.

Let stand at room temperature fifteen minutes, or cover and refrigerate overnight. Bake in a preheated oven at 350°F for forty-five minutes or until puffed and golden and knife inserted into the center of the strata comes out clean. Let rest for ten minutes, and serve hot.

Camille's Tip: If you are preparing this the night before and baking the next morning, be sure to take it out thirty minutes before baking so that it is room temperature.

Rye Crepes with Pastrami and Swiss

One day I came across a recipe for rye crepes, and I immediately thought of the creative opportunities that awaited! As I am a big fan of pastrami and Swiss on rye, I thought a crepe with these flavors would be a hit in the morning and especially for brunch. This is a standard rye crepe recipe that can be found on countless cooking web sites. I add the caraway seeds for an added kick.

3/4 cup rye flour

3/4 cup all-purpose flour

1 teaspoon salt

1 teaspoon baking powder

1 teaspoon caraway seeds

2 ¼ cup milk

1 egg

Vegetable oil

1 pound pastrami, sliced thin

1/2 pound Swiss cheese, shredded

In a large bowl, sift together first four ingredients. Add caraway seeds. Whisk the milk and egg together. Combine the dry and wet mixtures and stir well. Warm vegetable oil, starting with a tablespoon, in a sauté pan over medium heat. Spoon three tablespoons of batter onto the pan and carefully tilt it in a circular motion until the batter forms a round, thin crepe. Cook for one minute, and carefully flip the crepe over with a spatula. Cook for an additional thirty seconds. Repeat process with remaining batter.

Stack crepes in between wax paper. On a work surface, place a few folded slices of pastrami down the center of each crepe and sprinkle with Swiss cheese. Roll up. Place seam side down in a baking dish. Sprinkle top of each crepe with more Swiss cheese. Bake, uncovered, in a preheated oven at 350°F for 10 minutes or until Swiss cheese is melted.

Banana Breakfast Bake

Bananas are a great energy food in the morning. This particular recipe includes chocolate liqueur for a great morning kick, and it is especially great for a weekend morning when you have overnight company and a lot of plans for the day ahead.

4 whole bananas, peeled and sliced in rounds
1/4 cup butter, melted
2 tablespoons chocolate liqueur
1 tablespoon light cream
1 biscotti cookie, crushed to coarse crumbs

Layer the bananas on a greased baking dish or pan. Mix melted butter, chocolate liqueur, and light cream. Drizzle over bananas. Sprinkle with crushed biscotti cookie. Bake in a preheated oven at 350°F for about twenty-five minutes. Serve hot.

Camille's Tip: Rich in fiber, bananas are among the most popular fruits of prime athletes. For a boost and mood enhancer, top half a small bagel with banana slices and a bit of peanut butter for a great midday snack!

Sugared Walnut Bacon

The deep taste of this bacon, baked with the flavors of walnuts, brown sugar, and cinnamon, is so titillating that you can just eat it on its own along with a giant mug of coffee.

1 pound thick-sliced bacon
1/2 cup walnuts
1/2 cup light brown sugar
1 teaspoon ground cinnamon

Place a rack on top of a cookie sheet, and line bacon on the rack. Pulse walnuts in food processor until they are finely ground. In a bowl, combine walnuts, sugar, and cinnamon. Then, gently but firmly, press the walnut mixture onto the bacon. Bake in a preheated oven at 350°F for thirty minutes. Allow bacon to settle for five to ten minutes before serving.

Red, White, and Blue Breakfast Parfait

The fresh berries and the yogurt in this parfait are very invigorating as they come together in this recipe. I especially enjoy preparing this on Fourth of July weekend.

1/2 cup blueberries

1/2 cup sliced strawberries

2 tablespoons sugar

12 ounces vanilla yogurt

Mint for garnish

Toss berries with sugar and allow to sit for ten minutes. Add a spoonful of berries to the bottom of two parfait glasses, then a dollop of yogurt. Continue to alternately layer the ingredients. Garnish with mint.

Camille's Tip: Store yogurt on the cooler inside shelves of the refrigerator, not on the door shelves. This will keep it longer.

Pumpkin Smoothie

I adore anything pumpkin along with premium harvest flavors and spices. Every autumn, I whip up pumpkin recipes for pancakes, pies, cookies, and even cheesecakes! This particular pumpkin recipe is an unbeatable smoothie to make on an autumn day after a great workout or just to relax with the paper on a Sunday morning.

2 tablespoons canned pumpkin puree, chilled

1 cup milk

2 tablespoons sugar

1 teaspoon pumpkin spice

Ice cubes

Combine all ingredients into blender and mix on "smoothie" mode. Pour into chilled class, and sprinkle with a dash of cinnamon.

Camille's Tip: During autumn, using fresh pumpkin instead of canned is easy! Cut a pumpkin in half and bake, facedown, at 350°F for fifty minutes. Remove seeds and strings. Scoop out pumpkin pulp, down to the skin, and puree in a blender or food processor.

Appetizers and Fun Stuff

We go through life working our jobs and giving significant time to our careers so that we can reap the rewards, provide well for our families, be happy and fulfilled individuals, and enjoy all else that  life has to offer. Socializing, partying, and celebrating are some of the greatest pastimes for most of us. When we enjoy the festivities, it almost always begins with appetizers, hors d'oeuvres, finger foods, and generally fun edibles that are easy to pop into our mouths while we enjoy the addictive flavors. A variety of gratifying and refreshing drinks are an added bonus. The following recipes are some of my favorite appetizers and fun stuff that I enjoy serving to family and friends.

Chipotle Corn Fritters

Fritters are among my favorite finger foods. When I serve my corn fritters, I am told they are just scrumptious! These fritters can be made with just the corn if the Mexican ingredients do not fit in with the theme of the party. I also serve them as a side dish for a quick weeknight meal.

6 large ears of fresh corn on the cob, or two fifteen-ounce cans of corn
2 chipotle peppers in adobe sauce
2 eggs
3/4 cup Bisquick
1/4 cup fresh cilantro, chopped
Kosher salt and freshly ground black pepper
Vegetable oil

If you are using fresh corn, place the cobs on a hot grill and cook until lightly charred, turning frequently. On cutting board, cut the kernels from the cob, including the sweet milk in the cob that can be left behind in the cutting process. Drain excess adobe sauce from the chipotle peppers, and mince. In a bowl, mix the corn with the chipotle peppers, egg, Bisquick, cilantro, salt, and pepper.

In a sauté pan, warm vegetable oil over medium-high heat. Lower the heat to medium, and drop heaping spoonfuls of the corn batter into the hot oil. Do not overcrowd the fritters in the pan. Cook, turning once, until golden brown on both sides.

Garlic Shrimp with Vodka Cocktail Sauce

When I host a cocktail party, this is one of my favorite hors d'oeuvres to serve. I like to add a small spoonful of the vodka cocktail sauce onto an Asian hors d'oeuvre spoon, topped with a shrimp and garnished with curly parsley. The spoons sit attractively on a tray to be passed around to guests.

1 pound medium shrimp, peeled and deveined, with tails left on
2 garlic cloves, peeled and chopped
2 tablespoons butter, softened
2 tablespoons white wine
2 tablespoon extra-virgin olive oil
1 tablespoon fresh flat-leaf parsley, chopped
Kosher salt and freshly ground black pepper
1 cup cocktail sauce
2 tablespoons vodka
Zest of one lemon
1 tablespoon horseradish
1/8 teaspoon red pepper flakes

In a bowl, mix shrimp, garlic, butter, white wine, extra-virgin olive oil, parsley, salt, and pepper. Layer in a baking dish and bake, uncovered, in a preheated oven at 350°F for ten minutes. Allow to cool.

In a small bowl, mix cocktail sauce, vodka, lemon zest, horseradish, and red pepper flakes. Serve shrimps with cocktail sauce.

Roasted Scallops with Asian Chili Mayo

I first served these delightful scallops at a summer cocktail party on a Manhattan deck overlooking the water. Like the recipe for Garlic Shrimp with Vodka Cocktail Sauce, this is also a recipe that can be served on Asian hors d'oeuvre spoons. Just add a small dollop of the chili mayo onto the spoon, topped with a scallop and garnished with curly parsley.

1 pound scallops

2 garlic cloves, peeled and chopped

2 tablespoons butter, softened

2 tablespoons white wine

2 tablespoon extra-virgin olive oil

1 tablespoon flat-leaf parsley, chopped

Kosher salt and freshly ground black pepper

1 cup mayonnaise

1/2 cup Asian chili sauce

1/8 teaspoon red pepper flakes

In a bowl, mix scallops, garlic, butter, white wine, extra-virgin olive oil, parsley, salt, and pepper. Layer in a baking dish and bake, uncovered, in a preheated oven at 400°F for fifteen minutes. Allow to cool.

In a small bowl, mix mayonnaise, chili sauce and red pepper flakes. Serve scallops with with Asian chili mayonnaise

Shrimp Toast

These little shrimp toasts are another great party food. I recommend using Arnold's white bread, as it has a nice consistency.

1/2 pound shrimp, finely chopped
6 water chestnuts, finely chopped
1 egg, slightly beaten
Kosher salt and freshly ground black pepper
1/2 teaspoon ginger, grated
1 scallion, finely sliced
1 tablespoon sherry
Thin white bread
Vegetable oil

In a large bowl, mix all ingredients except for white bread and vegetable oil. Remove crust from white bread, and cut each slice into four triangular pieces. Spread shrimp mixture evenly on each triangle. In a large sauté pan, warm oil. Add each prepared toast, shrimp side down, four at a time, until golden. Flip over and fry on the bread side until toasted. Drain on paper towels, and serve piping hot.

Chorizo Mussels

I enjoy the marriage of chorizo and mussels so much that I created a recipe to bake them in the mussel's shell. This appetizer goes well with a glass of Pinot Noir or Pinot Grigio.

2 dozen mussels, scrubbed, beards removed
1/2 cup of clam juice
1 tablespoon extra-virgin olive oil
2 scallions
Vegetable oil
1/2 cup cooked chorizo sausage, finely chopped
1 tablespoon tomato paste
2 tablespoon fresh flat-leaf parsley, chopped
Kosher salt and freshly ground pepper

Bread Crumb Topping:
1 teaspoon garlic powder
1/3 cup bread crumbs
1 tablespoon melted butter
1 tablespoon olive oil
Fresh flat-leaf parsley, for garnish

Steam mussels in clam juice and olive oil until they are opened and cooked. Remove the mussels from the shells. Keep half the shells and discard the other half. Chop the mussels and the scallions. In a sauté pan, warm vegetable oil over medium heat. Add the scallions, mussels, chorizo, tomato paste, parsley, salt, and pepper. Stir a few minutes until mixed well and the flavors combine. Allow mixture to cool in a bowl.

Spoon the mixture into the shells. Mix the garlic powder, bread crumbs, melted butter, and olive oil until blended. Sprinkle bread crumb mixture over each mussel. Bake at 350°F until toasted. Garnish with parsley.

Camille's Tip: Do not be alarmed if the inside mussel meat is two different colors in your batch. Both are fresh and very edible. The pale white is a male mussel, while the yellow orange is female.

Crab Cakes

The recipes for crab cakes are many, and over the years, I have tried my fair share. By now, I have put together my own recipe that really works for me. When I had my crab cakes mastered, I started to make them on Christmas Eve for the Feast of Seven Fishes.

My mother made us all laugh as she showed her clear shock that I would serve a nontraditional seafood appetizer that was not of Italian origins. However, that very first Christmas Eve when serving those crab cakes, there was not a single one left on the platter!

1 ¼ cup very fine bread crumbs

1 pound jumbo lump crab

1/2 cup mayonnaise

2 egg whites

1 teaspoon Tabasco sauce

1 teaspoon fresh chives, chopped

2 teaspoons Dijon mustard

1 teaspoon Old Bay Seasoning

Canola oil

In a bowl, mix the bread crumbs, lump crab, mayonnaise, egg whites, Tabasco, chives, Dijon mustard, and Old Bay Seasoning. Gently mix with hands. Be careful to keep the jumbo crab in lump pieces. Form into crab cakes, and press tightly to hold ingredients together . You should get about nine or ten. Refrigerate for at least six hours, but overnight is even better.

In a sauté pan, warm canola oil over medium heat. Fry crab cakes in batches until golden, turning over once. Serve with lemon wedges or a favorite sauce.

Camille's Tips: People often have difficulty with their crab cakes falling apart. A few tips will aid in preventing that. Shape the crab cakes flat on your hand so that they are level. As suggested above, always chill them before frying. This will firm them up. Once they are shaped and chilled, handle them as little as possible. When frying, only turn them once.

Lobster Rolls

The glory of creamy lobster salad nestled in a warm buttery New England roll is priceless. There are a variety of recipes out there for lobster rolls, and there is also a bit of controversy over the best way to prepare them. In my opinion, whether you are eating one that hails from Maine or from a trendy metropolitan restaurant, you are destined to meet each taste with rich praise. The following recipe is how I prepare my lobster rolls.

2 pounds lobster meat, cooked and rough chopped
1 cucumber, peeled, seeded and chopped
3 tablespoons mayonnaise
1 tablespoon fresh-squeezed lemon juice
Dash of Tabasco sauce
1 tablespoon fresh flat-leaf parsley, chopped
1 teaspoon fresh chives, chopped
Kosher salt and freshly ground black pepper
8 split-top New England rolls (you may use split-top hot dog rolls)
Butter

In a bowl, mix lobster and cucumber. In a separate bowl, whisk mayonnaise, lemon juice and Tabasco. Add mayonnaise mixture to lobster and cucumber. Sprinkle in parsley, chives, salt and pepper . Gently mix to coat the lobster well. Open the rolls and brush with butter. Toast in oven until golden. Spoon lobster into each roll.

Memorable Mussels

When I was growing up, my father would take us to dinner at a local seafood house called Martini's. When entering Martini's, which was elegantly decorated in a fine nautical theme, it gave the promise of an exciting feast on the horizon. My sister Lucy and I always ordered an appetizer of chilled mussels. They were served with a refreshingly tangy dressing that I could not really define in ingredients during that youthful time of my life. However, the intense taste stayed with me after Martini's closed their doors for business a final time. Many years later, when I was catering a seafood dinner for a large group, I had a tremendous bag of mussels, and I wanted to create a new recipe to serve them. I thought about those chilled mussels at Martini's from days gone by. Now, as an experienced cook with many years of working food experience under my belt, I was able to accurately estimate the ingredients in that dressing. I tested it more than once and finally emerged with a dressing that matches the flavor Martini's would serve to their patrons.

1 shallot, diced

1 teaspoon Dijon mustard

2 tablespoons olive oil

1 tablespoon white vinegar

2 tablespoons maple syrup

Dash of Tabasco sauce

1 pound of mussels, steamed and chilled

Flat-leaf parsley

In a bowl, whisk the first six ingredients well. Arrange the chilled mussels on a platter and sprinkle a small amount of dressing on each mussel. Garnish with parsley. Serve chilled.

Shrimp Bruschetta

Ideas for bruschetta are endless, and I believe an entire cookbook can be written on the various ways to create it. My shrimp bruschetta is ambrosial in both appearance and flavor. The inspiration for this recipe comes to me from the ingredients I use for the Feast of the Seven Fishes every Christmas Eve.

1 8-ounce loaf French bread

3 tablespoons olive oil, divided

1 tablespoon fresh-squeezed lemon juice

1 tablespoon white vinegar

1 garlic clove, peeled and minced

1/2 pound cooked shrimp, chopped

1 tablespoon celery, diced

2 tablespoons sliced pitted black olives

1 tablespoon fresh flat-leaf parsley, chopped

Kosher salt and freshly ground black pepper

Cut bread into half-inch-thick slices. Brush both sides of each slice lightly with one tablespoon of the olive oil. Bake on a cookie sheet at 425°F until golden, turning over once.

In a medium bowl, mix remaining olive oil, lemon juice, white vinegar, and garlic. Add shrimp, celery, black olives, parsley, salt, and pepper and mix well. Spoon equal amounts of the shrimp mixture onto each toasted bruschetta slice and serve.

Camille's Tip: When serving any variation of bruschetta, always spoon your topping as close to serving time as possible. This will allow your guests to enjoy crunchy bruschetta, before the toasted bread becomes a bit soggy from the oil.

Honey Scallops Wrapped in Bacon

The next generation in my family especially enjoys my scallops. This can also be served with jumbo shrimp as a variation.

1/2 cup soy sauce

1 tablespoon orange juice

1/2 cup honey

2 tablespoons Dijon mustard

1 tablespoon brown sugar, plus more

1/8 teaspoon red pepper flakes

Kosher salt and freshly ground pepper

24 scallops

12 slices bacon

In a medium bowl, whisk soy sauce, orange juice, honey, Dijon mustard, brown sugar, red pepper flakes, salt, and pepper to create a marinade. Add scallops to the bowl of marinade and chill overnight or at least two hours.

Cut slices of bacon in half to make twenty-four shorter slices. Bake in oven at 350°F for six to eight minutes. Do not bake until crispy. Bacon should still be soft and easy to handle. Wrap a bacon slice around each scallop and secure with a toothpick. Layer in baking sheet and sprinkle with more brown sugar. Bake at 350°F for 20 minutes.

Tilapia Tacos

I prepared beef tacos for my sons for years. I also enjoy serving them for large festive gatherings. When hosting a casual party, I like to put all the toppings out on a display, and my guests can create their own taco with the toppings of their choice. I started to make tilapia tacos when I wanted to teach my culinary students that tacos can be made in many different ways. They have been a hit among family and friends ever since.

Spicy Tomato and Chipotle Dressing

1 plum tomato, diced

1 chipotle in adobe sauce

2 tablespoon Spanish onion, grated

2 tablespoons lime juice

1/4 cup canola oil

2 tablespoons cilantro, chopped

Dash of Tabasco sauce

Kosher salt and freshly ground pepper

Add all dressing ingredients to a food processor, give a few pulses, and set aside.

Tacos

12 hard corn taco shells

2 tablespoons canola oil

2 pounds tilapia, cut into finger-size pieces

1 teaspoon chili powder

1/2 teaspoon smoked paprika

1/4 teaspoon ground cumin

1/8 teaspoon garlic powder

1/8 teaspoon onion powder

1/8 teaspoon ground dried chipotle chili pepper

1 teaspoon salt

1 tablespoon cilantro

Half a head iceberg lettuce, shredded

Avocado slices

2 cups cheddar cheese, shredded

Sour cream

Warm taco shells in oven for ten minutes. While shells are warming, spread canola oil in baking dish or pan and layer tilapia slices. Mix chili powder, smoked paprika, cumin, garlic powder, onion powder, chipotle chili pepper, salt, and cilantro. Sprinkle over tilapia. Bake at 375°F for twelve minutes.

Cool the tilapia slightly, and divide it evenly among the warm taco shells. Garnish with the lettuce, avocado, cheddar cheese, sour cream, and spicy tomato chipotle dressing.

Savory Salmon Puffs

These puffs come out amazingly well every time I bake them. This recipe offers a salmon cheese filling, but you can go in any direction with these puffs, sweet or savory. You can also fill them with pudding or sweet custard.

Puffs:

1 cup water

1/2 cup vegetable shortening

1 cup flour

1/4 teaspoon, plus additional salt

5 eggs

Over medium heat, in a medium-size saucepan, bring water and shortening to a boil.

Add flour and stir well until mixture forms into a ball. Allow to cool. Add salt and four eggs, one at a time, beating well. On a lightly oiled cookie sheet, drop two-inch circles. Beat together the remaining egg and salt to create a glaze. With a pastry brush, gently brush the glaze on the tops of the dough. Bake at 425°F for twenty minutes. Then lower heat down to 350°F and bake for an additional twenty-five minutes.

Filling:

1 cup mascarpone cheese, softened

1/2 cup sour cream

1/4 cup smoked salmon, finely chopped

1 tablespoon horseradish

Dash of Tabasco sauce

1 tablespoon chopped dill

Freshly ground black pepper

Beat the mascarpone cheese and sour cream in a mixing bowl. Add smoked salmon, horseradish, Tabasco, dill, and black pepper. Carefully slice open the savory puffs horizontally and fill with the salmon mixture.

Prosciutto Pasta Pie

My mother served her pasta pie for many occasions. She would bake hers in a pot and make it with a dozen eggs and small round pasta called ditalini. My own version is one I have also been preparing for years. I prefer to use prosciutto, but you can substitute ham, salami, or pepperoni. This is an inviting brunch item, appetizer for dinner, or finger food for a party. Just cut into narrow wedges for easy noshing.

1 pound spaghetti
6 eggs
1/2 cup prosciutto, chopped
3/4 cup grated Pecorino Romano cheese, grated
1 cup mozzarella, shredded
1 tablespoon fresh flat-leaf parsley, chopped
Kosher salt and freshly ground black pepper
Vegetable oil
Butter

In a large pot, heat water for the pasta. When water begins to boil, add salt liberally. Let water return to a boil, and cook pasta to al dente. Drain well, and allow cooling.

Beat eggs very well, and add the prosciutto, Pecorino Romano, mozzarella, parsley, salt, and pepper. Add the spaghetti to the egg mixture, and mix well. In a large sauté pan, warm vegetable oil and butter over medium heat. Add the spaghetti-and-egg mixture. Cover and cook over low heat until the bottom is golden.

Slide the pie onto a plate, and add a bit more vegetable oil and butter to the sauté pan. Turn the pie over into the pan, and allow the other side to cook, uncovered, until golden. Allow pie to set for ten minutes, and cut into wedges, or use a round cutter and cut into circles. Serve with a simple arugula salad tossed in balsamic vinegar and extra-virgin olive oil.

Camille's Tip: This recipe can also be baked. Just mix the ingredients and pour into a buttered baking dish and bake at 350°F for thirty minutes.

Spicy Sausage Balls with Cherry Pepper Dip

My sausage balls are reminiscent of the old fashioned southern sausage cheese balls that have been popular for many decades, and they are easy and quick to make. They require no frying and just a simple fifteen minute bake.

1 pound loose sausage meat

2 cups Monterey Jack cheese, shredded

1 cup Bisquick

1 teaspoon chili powder
1/2 teaspoon smoked paprika
1/4 teaspoon ground cumin
1 teaspoon onion powder

In a large bowl, use your hands to mix sausage meat and Monterey Jack cheese very well. In a smaller bowl, whisk Bisquick, chili powder, smoked paprika, cumin and onion powder. Add Bisquck mixture to sausage bowl. With hands, mix all ingredients and roll sausage meat into one-inch balls. Place the balls on an ungreased baking sheet. Bake in a preheated oven at 350°F for fifteen minutes or until golden brown. Serve with cherry pepper dip.

Cherry Pepper Dip

1 cherry pepper

1 garlic clove

1 tablespoon cilantro, chopped

2 tablespoons olive oil

1 cup Greek yogurt

In a food processor, pulse the cherry pepper, garlic and cilantro while streaming in the olive oil. Stir cherry pepper mixture into Greek yogurt and mix well.

Grilled Hot Dogs and Spicy Onions

A festive topping of onions with rich flavors turns an ordinary hot dog into a fulfilling item for an outdoor party. You will find that your guests can't stop at one!

1/4 cup canola oil

1 tablespoon butter

2 large Spanish onions, sliced

2 tablespoon sugar

2 chipotles in adobe sauce, chopped

Kosher salt and freshly ground black pepper

1/4 cup ketchup

1 tablespoon cilantro, chopped

8 hot dogs, grilled

8 hot dog buns, toasted

In a sauté pan, warm canola oil and butter over medium heat. Add Spanish onions and cook until tender. Spoon in sugar to caramelize. Add chipotle and allow to cook for one minute. Stir in salt, pepper and ketchup, and allow flavors to combine. Toss in cilantro. Assemble hot dogs in toasted buns. Add a generous portion of onions to each hot dog.

Camille's Tip: I highly recommend organic hot dogs. The flavor is superior, and they are much healthier for us.

Sausage Wontons

I can just keep creating recipes with wonton wrappers over and over again. I was thrilled when I first found this wonderful ingredient in a charming gourmet market. When serving these wontons at a party, make a lot, as they are helplessly addictive.

1/2 pound loose sausage meat

1 shallot, chopped

1 cup ricotta, strained

1/4 cup shredded mozzarella

1/4 cup Pecorino Romano cheese, grated

2 tablespoons fresh basil, chopped

30 square wonton wrappers

1 egg white, lightly beaten

Vegetable oil

In a sauté pan, cook and stir sausage meat until no longer pink. Remove sausage, and cook the shallots in the same sauté pan, with sausage drippings, until tender. Drain any excess liquid, and allow both the sausage and shallots to cool.

In a medium bowl, combine the sausage, shallots, ricotta, mozzarella, Pecorino Romano cheese, and basil. Lay out wonton squares. Place a heaping teaspoon of the sausage mixture in the middle of each wonton, and brush the egg white along the edges. Gently fold over and firmly seal the edges of the wonton, forming a triangle. In a sauté pan, warm vegetable oil over medium-high heat. Fry wontons a few at a time, turning once, until golden. Serve warm.

Apple Wontons

In New York State, apple picking is a favored pastime. My three
sons and I would have a great time every autumn when we would go
on a day trip to the orchards. Such memories are my inspiration for
creating this simple apple wonton recipe.

2 medium apples, cored, peeled, and grated

2 cups ricotta, strained

1/4 cup sugar

1/4 teaspoon cinnamon

1 egg white, lightly beaten

20 square wonton wrappers

Vegetable oil

In a medium bowl, stir together apples, ricotta, sugar, and cinnamon
for filling. Lay out wonton squares. Place a generous teaspoon of
the apple-ricotta filling in the middle of each wonton, and brush the
egg white along the edges. Gently fold over and firmly seal the
edges of the wonton, forming a triangle. In a sauté pan, warm
vegetable oil over medium-high heat. Fry wontons a few at a time,
turning once, until golden. Serve warm.

Baked Brie and Pineapple in a Puff Pastry

My brie and pineapple baked in puff pastry is always the first item to be consumed on my buffet table, and it was an item that I offered very often on my catering menu. When I serve this I make the first cut so that the savory brie comes oozing out of the flaky puff pastry along with the sweet and warm pineapple.

1 puff pastry sheet, thawed

1 8-ounce round of brie cheese

1/2 cup of pineapple preserves

1 teaspoon chives, chopped

1 egg, beaten

On a floured work surface, lay out the pastry sheet. Place the brie in the center. Mix pineapple preserves and chives and spoon on top of brie cheese. Fold the pastry up over the cheese and twist into a seal. Brush the pastry puff with the egg. Bake in a preheated oven at 350°F for twenty-five minutes or until golden brown. Allow to settle for ten minutes. Serve warm with gourmet crackers

Avocado Butter with Paprika Toast

This mellow spread is a great comfort food while offering the terrific nutritional values of fresh green avocados and one of my favorite herbs, cilantro.

1 ripe avocado

5 ounces of butter, softened

1 tablespoon fresh-squeezed lime juice

Zest from half a lemon

1 teaspoon fresh cilantro, finely chopped

8 slices fresh egg bread

Paprika Kosher salt and freshly ground black pepper

Mix avocado, butter, lime juice, lemon zest and cilantro until smooth. Chill for 30 minutes. Remove crust from egg bread. Toast the bread slices and cut into triangle shapes. Sprinkle with paprika. Serve the avocado butter with the warm egg bread slices

Camille's Tip: For a more attractive presentation, you may cut the egg bread toast into circles with a round cutter.

Eggplant Balls

Even friends who are not fans of eggplant always enjoy this gratifying appetizer. They pop right into your mouth, and they are very irresistible.

1 whole eggplant, peeled and sliced

Table salt

3/4 cup seasoned bread crumbs

1 egg, beaten

3 garlic cloves, grated

1 cup Pecorino Romano cheese, grated

2 tablespoon fresh flat-leaf parsley, minced

1 tablespoon fresh mint, minced

Vegetable oil

Marinara Sauce (page 227)

Lightly salt each side of the eggplant slices, and place them in a colander. Layer a sheet of plastic wrap or aluminum foil on top of the eggplant slices, and place a large, heavy can on top for about one hour. Allow any excess water to drain from the eggplant.

Place the eggplant slices on a baking sheet, and bake until cooked, about twenty-five minutes. Coarsely chop the eggplant. Batches at a time, place the eggplant in a food processor at a medium pulse. Do not over-pulse. Place the eggplant in a bowl, and add remaining ingredients, mixing well. Roll the eggplant mixture into walnut-sized balls.

In a sauté pan, warm oil over medium heat. Fry the eggplant balls, turning, until golden. Serve with marinara sauce.

Camille's Tip: When buying eggplants, always choose one that feels light. Heavier eggplants have a lot of seeds, which may yield a bitter taste.

Mexican Pizza Squares

When I would present cooking demonstrations, I would teach my audience how to make pizza. After a while, I wanted to bring a different twist to my demonstration, so I prepared these Mexican pizza squares. Everyone responded very favorably to the Mexican flavors and ingredients baked into the homemade dough, thus making this an instant hit.

Pizza Dough:

2 envelopes active dry yeast

1 cup warm water, 110–115 degrees

1 teaspoon salt

2 teaspoons sugar

2 tablespoons olive oil

3 1/2 cups flour

In a large bowl, dissolve yeast and warm water. Stir in salt, sugar and half the olive oil. Gradually add flour and mix ingredients until dough forms. Turn the dough out onto a floured surface and knead for about five minutes, until firm. Rub remaining olive oil in a bowl. Place the dough in the oiled bowl and turn around to coat all sides. Cover with plastic wrap and a dish towel, and place the dough in a warm spot. Allow to rise until doubled in size.

Camille's Tip: Whenever forming a dough, do not overwork it, as the dough will toughen.

Topping:

2 tablespoons extra-virgin olive oil

1 firm, ripe vine tomato

$1^1/_2$ cup cheddar cheese, shredded

2 garlic cloves, peeled and diced

3 chipotle peppers

2 tablespoons cilantro, chopped

Roll out pizza dough into a rectangle shape and form onto a rectangular pizza stone or a baking sheet. Brush the olive oil onto the dough. Slice the tomatoes and arrange over the dough. Sprinkle the cheddar cheese onto the tomatoes. Dice the chipotle peppers and add over the cheese. Sprinkle the cilantro over the entire pizza.

Bake in a preheated oven at 400°F for twenty minutes or until bottom of the pizza is a golden brown. Allow to settle for a few minutes. Cut the pizza into two-by-two-inch squares and serve.

Camille's Tip: Invest in a well-made pizza baking stone. It distributes heat evenly and yields a great crust to the bottom of a pizza.

Pineapple Fritters

These sweet, fluffy fritters do not even make it to the serving table when I am frying them. They are finished off by my family as I transfer them from the sauté pan to the platter.

2 cups of crushed pineapple, drained
2 eggs
3/4 cup Bisquick
1 tablespoon sugar
1/4 cup fresh mint, chopped
Vegetable oil
Confectioners' sugar

In a bowl, mix the pineapple, egg, Bisquick, sugar and mint. In a sauté pan, warm vegetable oil over medium-high heat. Lower the heat to medium, and drop heaping spoonfuls of the pineapple batter into the hot oil. Do not overcrowd them in the pan. Cook, turning once, until golden brown on both sides. Dust with confectioners' sugar and serve.

Polenta

Many years ago, my courage in tackling polenta came from the fact that my father loves it. I often make it for him on Father's Day along with our cookout food. Polenta can remain a vegetarian dish, or you can lightly top it with a spicy sausage tomato sauce. Always add a liberal amount of grated cheese.

$5^1/_2$ cups water
1 tablespoon table salt
$1^3/_4$ cups cornmeal
Parmigiano-Reggiano cheese, grated

In a large pot, bring water to a boil. Add salt. Gradually stir in the cornmeal. Lower heat, and stir for about twenty-five minutes, until the mixture thickens. Pour polenta into a baking dish or pan and allow to settle. Sprinkle a very generous amount of Parmigiano-Reggiano cheese. Add marinara sauce. Cut into squares to serve.

Camille's Tip: Polenta is best cooked with water, as milk or chicken stock can take away from the flavor of the corn.

Spicy Fried Chickpeas

Fun, nutty, and peppery--those are the words to sum up my chickpeas. Toss these down with an ice-cold longneck of beer, and it will be one great picnic, party, Super Bowl, or maybe just a night on the couch, for two, watching a movie.

1 pound dry chickpeas
Vegetable oil, for deep-frying
1/2 teaspoon garlic powder
1/4 teaspoon cayenne pepper
2 teaspoons cilantro, chopped

In a bowl, cover the chickpeas with cold water and refrigerate overnight. Drain well and pat dry. Add enough oil in a deep pan to deep-fry the chickpeas. Deep-fry the chick peas in batches until golden brown. Drain well. Mix the garlic powder, cayenne pepper, and cilantro and toss with the chickpeas. Serve cool.

Beer Dip

Place a round bowl of this robust dip right into the center of the other dips, and it will be the star. I have received raves on this time and again.

8 ounces cream cheese

1/4 cup sour cream

1/4 cup cheddar cheese, shredded

1/4 cup Monterey Jack cheese, shredded

2 scallions, sliced

1/4 cup light beer

1/2 cup black olives, sliced

1 teaspoon poppy seeds

Allow cream cheese to soften. In a bowl, combine all ingredients. Mix well. Serve with crackers.

Camille's Bloody Mary

My particular version of this popular cocktail comes with a twist to reflect my upbringing in Italian food.

1/2 cup packed fresh basil

1/2 cup beef stock

1 cup of cherry tomatoes

3 cups ice

2 tablespoons fresh-squeezed lemon

1/2 teaspoon crushed red pepper flakes

3/4 cup vodka

6 cups tomato juice

1 tablespoon Worcestershire sauce

1 tablespoon horseradish

Celery stalks for garnish

In a blender, puree basil, beef stock and cherry tomatoes very well. In a pitcher, combine ice, lemon, red pepper flakes, vodka, tomato juice, Worcestershire sauce and horseradish. Mix well. Add cherry tomato mixture. Serve in chilled Collins glasses and garnish with celery and basil leaves.

Camille's Tip: As tomato juice is the main ingredient of any Bloody Mary, always use a richly flavored, high-quality brand.

Peach Bellini

Prosecco is the original wine used to create a Bellini. However, I recommend prosecco spumante because, unlike the original prosecco, it is fermented a second time. This means it will not grow stale and it yields more "fizz" action, and that makes this drink exciting. This variation is a bit more costly, but very worth the expense.

4 ounces white peaches, pureed
Ice cubes
16 ounces prosecco spumante
Grenadine (optional)

Add ice cubes and evenly divided amounts of peach puree to four chilled champagne flutes. Pour the champagne and allow to fizz. Add a shot of grenadine to each flute for a nice splash of color.

Camille's Tip: If you wish to make a Bellini when ripe white peaches are not in season, then you may substitute with peach nectar.

Rainbow Virgin Cocktail

This is my very colorful and attractive way to serve a nonalcoholic drink for any party time. It especially allows the designated drivers of the evening to enjoy a tasty and festive drink.

$1^3/_4$ cup orange juice
$1^3/_4$ cup cranberry juice
Cold seltzer
1 orange, sliced in rounds
1 lime, sliced in rounds
1 lemon, sliced in rounds
Mint

Pour orange juice to fill an empty ice cube tray and place in freezer. Repeat with cranberry juice. When ice cubes are ready, place in a chilled pitcher. Add seltzer, oranges, limes, and lemons. Serve in chilled glasses with a garnish of mint.

Mango Mimosa

"Meeting Franklin Roosevelt was like opening our first bottle of champagne; knowing him was like drinking it." ~Winston Churchill

Among the many quotes to read, this is one of my favorites. I am sure Roosevelt was quite the man, and how interesting that Churchill would compare him to champagne. To me, champagne in a mimosa is what gracious living is all about. My first mimosa was at the wedding of my cousins Louis and Dolores, when I was a teenager. They were married in a ceremony on the water, and afterward we celebrated their union with a brunch reception. I still recall the beautiful weather and all the ladies in their summer dresses while we sipped the tangy flutes of mimosa. Louis and Dolores recently celebrated twenty-five years of marriage. This mimosa recipe is for them!

4 ounces mango nectar
1 teaspoon fresh-squeezed lemon juice
16 ounces sparkling wine or champagne
Slices of lime for garnish

Add even divided amounts of mango nectar and lemon juice to four chilled champagne flutes. Pour the champagne and allow to fizz. Garnish flutes with a slice of lime.

Camille's Tip: Do not throw away the cork of the champagne or wine bottle. Save it to place on the tip of a sharp knife that you keep in your kitchen drawer. This is a great way to maintain a safe kitchen environment.

Orange Sherbet Mimosa

"Orange is the happiest color." ~Frank Sinatra

There is no dispute that bright orange brings a smile to our face and especially to our food. This is my little twist on the traditional mimosa. Just add a spoon of sherbet for that added kick.

4 ounces orange juice
Ice cubes
4 teaspoons orange sherbet
16 ounces champagne
Orange slices

Add evenly divided amounts of orange juice to four chilled champagne flutes. Add two ice cubes to each flute, and a teaspoon of orange sherbet. Pour the champagne and allow to fizz. Garnish each glass with a slice of orange.

Sangria

The relaxing summer days of July and August calls for sweet and chilled home-made sangria. The good news is that we can make sangria every day of the week and never use the same recipe! It is best to use a tasty, inexpensive table wine, and although a robust burgundy is usually the preferred choice for sangria, you can also use white wine. The versatility of sangria is that you can add any combination of fruit to your liking, but be sure to use a fruity wine that will be able to support the additional fruit ingredients. Your wine shop owner can guide you on the structure and particulars of any chosen wine that will best match the fruits you wish to include. When creating white sangria, you may include white peaches and peach schnapps, or add a variety of berries to a robust Zinfandel. The possibilities are endless.

1 orange, sliced

1 lemon, sliced

1 apple, cubed

1 cup strawberries, halved

1/4 cup sugar

1 bottle of fruity red table wine

1 cup club soda (optional)

Ice

Mix fruits, sugar, and wine very well. Chill overnight. Add club soda, if desired, and ice right before serving.

Camille's Tip: Apples should always be cubed in sangria. Wine is acidic and will break down the apples if sliced too thin. This can also happen with peaches, so always cut your peaches thick when using them in sangria.

Salads and Soups

Our salads and our soups! I have rarely met any one person who dislikes either or both. The great thing about them is that there is such an opportunity for variation. For our salads, I shun any "rules" out there in the culinary world. My advice is to enjoy your salads as you please. Toss your favorite ingredients in a bowl, and add a lively dressing of your choice. For soups, allow them to comfort you. A nice warm bowl of soup with tangy flavors of vegetables, meats, and seasonings is an unbeatable option after a

long day. A cold gazpacho is also a great lunch or light dinner in the summer. When cooking soups, it is very acceptable to use store-bought soup stock in the many varieties that are sold, chicken, beef, fish, or vegetable. However, for an intense and deeply rich flavor, there is no comparison to making your own stock right in your kitchen. Stock works very well when frozen and thawed. I suggest preparing it in a large quantity and then freezing it in plastic Ziploc bags for easy thawing. You may also freeze part of the stock in an ice cube tray for when you need only a small amount in a given recipe.

Beef Tips and Romaine Salad with Tequila Dressing

Adding beef tips is a refreshing change from the usual grilled chicken breast that often tops a salad. The addition of the tequila also adds a nice twist to this salad that makes for a great meal in itself for a summer dinner.

6 ounces beef tenderloin tips
Kosher salt and freshly ground black pepper
1 tablespoon extra-virgin olive oil, plus 1/2 cup for dressing
2 cups romaine lettuce, torn
1/2 cup celery, chopped
1 tablespoon tomato juice
1 tablespoon fresh-squeezed lemon juice
2 teaspoons tequila
1 tablespoon flat-leaf parsley, finely chopped

Layer beef tenderloin tips on a clean work surface, sprinkle with salt and pepper, and drizzle with one tablespoon of olive oil. Grill on medium-high heat for five minutes, turning once. Allow meat to rest to room temperature.

In a large bowl, combine romaine lettuce and celery. In smaller bowl, whisk tomato juice, lemon juice, tequila, parsley, extra-virgin olive oil, salt, and pepper. Toss with salad ingredients, and top with beef tenderloin tips.

Camille's Tip: This salad and dressing can also be prepared with grilled shrimp.

Watercress and Peach Salad

Watercress is one of my favorite greens to use in a salad. It is crisp and refreshing, and it reminds me of a brilliant spring or summer day. The peaches in this particular salad add a nice sweetness to the peppery flavor of the watercress. I like to serve this with tall, cold glasses of iced tea.

2 teaspoons champagne vinegar

2 tablespoons extra-virgin olive oil

1/2 tablespoon onion, grated

Kosher salt and freshly ground black pepper

2 bunches watercress

2 tablespoons sliced almonds

1/4 cup fresh peaches, cubed

In a small bowl, whisk together the champagne vinegar, oil, onion and salt and pepper. Pour the vinaigrette over the watercress and toss well. Garnish with almonds and peaches.

Tomato Kirby Poppy Seed Salad

This particular salad always satisfies the craving for a crunchy and refreshing lunch. It is also very colorful.

4 ripe plum tomatoes, quartered
2 Kirby cucumbers, peeled and sliced
1 teaspoon sugar
2 tablespoons white vinegar
1/4 teaspoon dry mustard
1 tablespoon onion, grated
Kosher salt and freshly ground black pepper
1/2 cup vegetable oil
1 tablespoon poppy seeds

Place tomatoes and Kirbys in a large bowl. In a small bowl, whisk remaining ingredients to create a poppy seed dressing. Add dressing to the tomatoes and cucumbers, and toss well to coat.

Avocado Salad with Honey Lime Dressing

I have been preparing fresh avocado salad since I was a teenager. When I was growing up, my parents were never fans of avocado, so I very much discovered this on my own when I started to explore in fruit and vegetable markets.

2 medium ripe avocados

1/2 medium red onion, thinly sliced

1 tablespoon dill

1 garlic clove, peeled and diced

2 tablespoons fresh-squeezed lime juice

2 teaspoons raw honey

2 tablespoons extra-virgin olive oil

Kosher salt and freshly ground black pepper

Place the avocado on a cutting board. Cut through the center of the avocado, lengthwise, until the knife comes in contact with the side of the pit. Without removing the knife, cut in a circular motion around the pit, until the knife makes a full turn to the beginning incision point. Keep the knife in place and twist slightly to separate the two halves. One half will still have a large pit in the middle. Carefully, strike the pit with the blade of the knife with just enough force so the knife is embedded in the pit. When you raise the knife, the pit will come out of the avocado half. Spoon the avocado pulp away from the skin. Cut the pulp into lengthwise slices and transfer to a bowl. Add the red onion and dill.

In another bowl, mix the garlic, lime juice, honey, olive oil, salt, and pepper. Whisk well. Gently toss all ingredients together, lightly coating the avocados.

Bean Dijon Salad

My father, a fitness guru and a professional massage therapist, would always make his own version of a healthy three-bean salad. Eventually, we would affectionately call it "Grandpa's Bean Salad." Over the years, I redeveloped it with a few more ingredients. It is light and colorful and a great addition for any summer barbecue.

1 cup canned pinto beans

1 cup canned black beans

1 cup canned chickpeas

1 cup canned navy beans

1/3 cup red bell pepper, chopped

1/3 cup orange bell pepper, chopped

1/3 cup yellow bell pepper, chopped

2 scallions, chopped

2 garlic cloves, peeled and chopped

2 tablespoon fresh-squeezed lemon juice

2 tablespoon red wine vinegar

1 tablespoon Dijon mustard

1/3 cup extra-virgin olive oil

1 tablespoon flat-leaf parsley, chopped

Kosher salt and freshly ground black pepper, to taste

Drain the beans in a colander and rinse well. Shake out all excess water. Mix beans in a large bowl with red, orange, and yellow peppers, scallions, and garlic. Whisk the lemon juice, vinegar, Dijon mustard, and olive oil. Sprinkle in parsley, salt, and pepper. Toss all the ingredients together. Serve chilled.

Tricolor Salad with Gorgonzola Cheese, Walnuts, and Fig Dressing

Arugula, endive, and radicchio make for a very colorful salad with a peppery bite, and I especially enjoy serving it with the flavors of figs and gorgonzola cheese. The savory and sweet flavors create a great combination.

1 bunch arugula

2 endives, spears separated

1 small head radicchio, julienned

Half a medium red onion, thinly sliced

1 tablespoon fig jam

1/4 cup champagne vinegar

1/3 cup extra-virgin olive oil

Kosher salt and freshly ground black pepper

1/4 cup crumbled gorgonzola cheese

1/4 cup walnuts, toasted

In a large bowl, add arugula, endives, radicchio, and red onion. Whisk fig jam, champagne vinegar and extra-virgin olive oil. Toss with salad ingredients, and add salt and pepper. Top with gorgonzola cheese and walnuts.

Camille's Tip: Always store nuts in the freezer. This will keep them from turning rancid due to their high fat content.

Curry and Ginger Chicken Salad

My addition of curry powder and fresh ginger breathes new life to a traditional chicken salad. I especially like to serve this at a cocktail party as it adds a nice variety to my list of hors d'oeuvres.

1 pound chicken cutlets

Olive oil

Kosher salt and freshly ground black pepper

3/4 cup mayonnaise

$1^1/_2$ tablespoons curry powder

1 teaspoon fresh ginger, grated

1/2 cup toasted almond slivers

Choice of lettuce cups or crackers

Arrange chicken cutlets on a baking sheet. Brush with olive oil, and sprinkle with salt and pepper, liberally. Bake at 350°F for twenty minutes, until the chicken is just cooked. Remove from oven, and allow to cool. Cut chicken into small chunks and place in bowl. Add mayonnaise, curry powder, ginger, and almonds. Mix well, and serve chilled in lettuce cups or with crackers.

Thanksgiving Friday Turkey Salad

If you visit my home on Friday, the day after Thanksgiving, this is what I will be serving for lunch. I think I enjoy making this turkey salad more than I enjoy the turkey dinner on Thanksgiving Day! Always serve it chilled.

2 cups of cooked turkey, cubed
1/4 cup celery, diced
1 tablespoon fresh flat-leaf parsley, chopped
1/2 cup mayonnaise
2 tablespoons fresh-squeezed lemon juice
Kosher salt and freshly ground black pepper
2 endives, spears separated

In a bowl, mix all ingredients well, excluding the endive. Separate endive and arrange on a platter to use as cups. Fill each endive cup with the turkey salad, and chill for thirty minutes.

Camille's Tip: This turkey salad is another great addition for a cocktail party. Top spoonfuls on cucumber slices and serve as an hors d'oeuvre.

Creamy Potato Salad

Thanks to my dad, who handed this recipe down to me, my entire family enjoys this creamy potato salad at our barbeque cookouts and many parties.

5 pounds red potatoes

$1^1/_4$ cup celery, chopped

2 hard-boiled eggs, chopped

1 cup mayonnaise

1/4 cup spicy brown mustard

1/2 cup heavy cream

1/4 cup white vinegar

Kosher salt and freshly ground black pepper

Paprika

Fresh flat-leaf parsley, chopped

Peel and cut potatoes into medium size cubes. Place them in a pot, and add just enough cold water to cover. Bring to a boil, and lower to simmer for another five minutes. Potatoes should be cooked all the way through, but still firm. Drain the potatoes well in a colander. Cool potatoes after boiling, and mix gently with celery and hard-boiled eggs in a large bowl. In a smaller bowl, whisk mayonnaise, mustard, heavy cream, white vinegar, salt, and pepper. Add wet ingredients into potato bowl, and gently toss until all ingredients are combined well. Serve chilled, and garnish with paprika and parsley.

Chicken Stock

Chicken stock is the foundation for a knock-out chicken soup, but it also lends an uncomplicated lift to countless recipes while allowing the main ingredients to shine.

1 whole chicken, about 4 pounds

3 carrots, cut in large chunks

4 celery stalks, cut in large chunks

2 large yellow onions, unpeeled and quartered

1 head of garlic, halved

10 sprigs fresh dill

10 sprigs fresh flat-leaf parsley

5 sprigs fresh thyme

2 bay leaves

1 teaspoon whole black peppercorns

1 tablespoon kosher salt

Rinse the chicken, and discard giblets. Place chicken, along with remaining ingredients, in a large stockpot. Fill with cold water only high enough to cover the chicken. On high heat, bring to a quick boil for a few minutes. Turn heat down to medium-low, and gently simmer for three hours. When foam rises to the top, skim off with a spoon. If needed, add hot water to keep ingredients submerged. Carefully strain the stock through a colander covered with a cheesecloth. Press the solid ingredients into the cheesecloth in order to release the juices. Cool immediately by placing the stockpot in a sink of ice water. Chill in refrigerator overnight. Remove the surface fat from the top of the liquid. Use stock within three days or place in freezer.

Camille's Tip: Always remove the leaves from the celery. They are bitter in flavor and not beneficial to a stock.

Beef Stock

Beef stock is actually a variety of brown stock, and this is what we use when seeking deep flavor for our soups and stews. Brushing tomato paste and roasting the bones yields the rich brown color to the stock.

5 pounds of beef bones and veal bones mixed (ask your butcher to saw them in half)

1/2 cup tomato paste

3 carrots, cut in large chunks

4 celery stalks, cut in large chunks

2 large yellow onions, unpeeled and quartered

1 head of garlic, halved

10 sprigs fresh flat-leaf parsley

5 sprigs fresh thyme

2 bay leaves

1 teaspoon whole black peppercorns

1 tablespoon kosher salt

Rinse bones in cold water and pat dry. Brush with tomato paste. Place bones in large roasting pan and roast in a preheated oven at 450°F for thirty minutes, turning once. Arrange carrots, celery, and onions over bones and roast another thirty minutes.

Deglaze the roasting pan by adding one cup of water. Stir to scrape up browned bits, and cook over medium heat for a few minutes. Add the deglazed liquid, bones, carrots, celery, onions, and remaining ingredients in a large pot. Add water only high enough to cover the ingredients. On high heat, bring to a quick boil for a few minutes. Turn heat down to medium-low and gently simmer for three hours.

When foam rises to the top, skim off with a spoon. If needed, add hot water to keep ingredients submerged. Carefully strain the stock through a colander covered with a cheesecloth. Press the solid ingredients into the cheesecloth in order to release the juices. Cool immediately by placing the stockpot in a sink of ice water. Chill in refrigerator overnight. Remove the surface fat from the top of the liquid. Use within three days or place in freezer.

Camille's Tip: Only use a tablespoon of salt in a stock. This will prevent over salting when you use the stock in a recipe.

Fish Stock

Fish stock is an excellent foundation for seafood soups, sauces, chowders, and risotto. The best fish bones to use are those from mild, lean whitefish such as halibut, cod, or flounder. Avoid oily fish such as salmon, trout, or mackerel, as they contain too much fat to make a nice clean stock.

2 tablespoons vegetable oil

3 carrots, chopped

4 celery stalks, chopped

1 large yellow onion, unpeeled and quartered

1 small head of fennel, chopped

3 pounds of fish bones and heads

1 cup dry white wine

1 head of garlic, halved

10 sprigs fresh dill

10 sprigs fresh flat-leaf parsley

5 sprigs fresh thyme

2 lemons, sliced

2 bay leaves

1 teaspoon whole black peppercorns

1 tablespoon kosher salt

In a large stockpot, warm the vegetable oil over medium heat. Add the carrots, celery, onion, and fennel. Stirring frequently, cook until the vegetables become very soft, without browning. Add the fish ingredients and wine. Cook until bones appear white, without browning. Add remaining ingredients.

Fill stockpot with cold water only high enough to cover the contents. On high heat, bring to a quick boil for a few minutes. Turn heat down to medium low, and gently simmer for forty minutes.

When foam rises to the top, skim off with a spoon. Carefully strain the stock through a colander covered with a cheesecloth. Press the solid ingredients into the cheesecloth in order to release the juices. Cool immediately by placing the stockpot in a sink of ice water. Chill in refrigerator overnight. Remove the surface fat from the top of the liquid. Use within three days or place in freezer.

Vegetable Stock

The following recipe is for a basic vegetable stock, but you can include just about any vegetable you wish. You can also include vegetable scraps such as asparagus ends, clean potato peels, and broccoli and cauliflower stems.

2 tablespoons vegetable oil

3 carrots, chopped

4 celery stalks, chopped

2 large yellow onions, unpeeled and quartered

1 small head of fennel, chopped

1 medium leek, sliced and rinsed well, tough outer leaves removed

1 cup button mushrooms, sliced

2 ripe red vine tomatoes, cut in quarters

1 head of garlic, halved

10 sprigs fresh dill

10 sprigs fresh flat-leaf parsley

10 sprigs fresh basil

5 sprigs fresh thyme

2 bay leaves

1 teaspoon whole black peppercorns

1 tablespoon kosher salt

In a large stockpot, warm the vegetable oil over medium heat. Add the carrots, celery, onion, fennel, and leeks. Stirring frequently, cook until the vegetables become soft, without browning. Add remaining ingredients, and fill pot with cold water. On high heat, bring to a quick boil for a few minutes. Turn heat down to medium low, and gently simmer for thirty minutes.

When foam rises to the top, skim off with a spoon. Carefully strain the stock through a colander covered with a cheesecloth. Press the solid ingredients into the cheesecloth in order to release the juices. Cool immediately by placing the stockpot in a sink of ice water. Chill in refrigerator overnight. Remove the surface fat from the top of the liquid. Use within three days or place in freezer.

Shallot Cream Soup

I just have a love affair with shallots. They are one of my favorite ingredients. Onions get so much attention when it comes to soups, and so I created my own soup with shallots as the star. Shallots have a much softer taste than onions, and this will allow for a mellow and pleasant flavor to the soup.

3 tablespoons extra-virgin olive oil

3 tablespoons butter

6 shallots, chopped

2 garlic cloves, peeled and chopped

2 sprigs fresh thyme

2 bay leaves

Kosher salt and freshly ground black pepper

1 cup dry white wine

2 quarts beef stock

1 cup heavy cream

2 tablespoons brandy

In a large pot, warm olive oil and butter over medium heat. Add shallots and cook until tender. Add garlic, thyme, bay leaves, salt, and pepper. Stir in the white wine, and cook for one minute. Add beef stock and heavy cream, and simmer on medium-low heat for forty-five minutes. When soup is done, remove bay leaves and thyme and stir in brand

Pancetta and Butternut Squash Soup

Butternut squash soup is such a common crowd-pleaser. As always, I looked for a different twist on creating a dish. The addition of the pancetta to this soup laces the taste of the butternut squash superbly.

2 tablespoons extra-virgin olive oil

2 cups pancetta, diced

7 cups butternut squash, chopped

6 garlic cloves, peeled and chopped

Kosher salt and freshly ground black pepper

6 cups vegetable stock

1 cup half-and-half

In a large pot, warm olive oil over medium heat. Add pancetta, and cook, stirring occasionally, until crisp. Using a slotted spoon, transfer the pancetta to a plate lined with a paper towel.

Add the butternut squash, garlic, salt, and pepper to the pancetta drippings. Cook for ten minutes, stirring occasionally. Add the vegetable stock, and cook until the butternut squash is tender. Add half the pancetta.

Working in batches, transfer the soup to a food processor or blender and puree the soup. You may also use an immersion blender. Return the soup to the pot. Add the rest of the pancetta, and whisk in the half-and-half. Simmer another ten minutes.

Camille's Tip: For easier dicing, place pancetta in the freezer for about fifteen minutes.

Italian Wedding Soup

The interesting news is that I have never seen Italian Wedding Soup served at one Italian wedding, and I have been to countless such events. Contrary to what many would think, the name of this soup did not develop due to a presence at the happy occasion of marriage. Rather, it is called wedding soup because the ingredients, to many Italians, are a perfect marriage of meat and vegetables in a delicate broth.

I have been enjoying this soup for a long time, and it is certainly a favorite. I use acini de pepe which is a small round pasta, but you can certainly use any small pasta of your choice.

Meatballs

1 cup seasoned bread crumbs

1 pound of ground beef

1 cup Pecorino Romano cheese, grated

1 egg

1/4 cup fresh flat-leaf parsley, minced

4 garlic cloves, peeled

1/4 cup extra-virgin olive oil

Kosher salt and freshly ground black pepper

In a large bowl, mix bread crumbs, ground beef, Pecorino Romano cheese, egg, and parsley, salt and pepper. Press garlic cloves through a garlic presser and add to mixture. Mix all ingredients until well blended. Roll into baby meatballs. In a large soup pot, warm olive oil over medium heat and brown the meatballs. Remove meatballs and set aside.

Soup

One medium onion, diced

2 teaspoons chicken base

2 cups of fresh escarole, cleaned and chopped

Kosher salt and freshly ground black pepper

2 1/2 quarts chicken stock

1 cup Pecorino Romano grated cheese

Acini de pepe

In the same large soup pot used to brown the meatballs, add onion to the drippings and cook until tender. Mix in chicken base and allow to dissolve well. Add escarole and stir as greens start to wilt down into the onions. Sprinkle in salt and pepper. Pour in the chicken stock and simmer for 30 minutes. Add meatballs and allow to simmer another 15 minutes. In a second pot, boil water for the acini de pepe. When water begins to boil, add salt liberally. Let water return to a boil. Add acini de pepe, and cook until al dente. Drain and add to soup along with Pecorino Romano cheese.

Zucchini Egg Drop Soup

Some people consider zucchini the lost and forgotten vegetable. That is the reason why I am so proud of this soup. My great-grandmother passed down her simpler version of zucchini soup, and since then, I've recreated it.

1/2 cup olive oil
1 large yellow onion, chopped
2 large zucchini, chopped
2 quarts vegetable stock
2 tablespoons fresh flat-leaf parsley, chopped
1 tablespoon fresh mint, chopped
Kosher salt and freshly ground black pepper
Tabasco
2 large eggs, beaten well
$1^1/_2$ cups Parmigiano-Reggiano cheese, grated

In a large pot, warm olive oil over medium heat. Add yellow onion and zucchini. Cook for three minutes. Add vegetable stock, parsley, mint, salt, and pepper. Add a few shots of Tabasco to taste. Simmer for forty-five minutes. Remove pot from heat, drizzle the beaten egg from fingertips, clockwise, while stirring the soup in the same direction, so that it will create threads of egg. Add Parmigiano-Reggiano cheese, and stir.

Chicken Ravioli Soup

I adore chicken soup, and I would serve steaming bowls of it in my restaurant daily. At home, I will sit with a bowl and work at whatever project I am involved with at the moment. Many times, I add a pasta such as ditalini or acini di pepe. You can find either in the boxed pasta section of your grocer. However, when serving this for guests, there is nothing like mini ravioli, or even tortellini, filled with ricotta to complement the flavors of the soup. You can find mini ravioli in the frozen section of your supermarket.

1 whole roasted chicken, 3 to 4 pounds

3 celery stalks, chopped

3 carrots, chopped

1 medium onion, chopped

2 tablespoons fresh thyme

2 quarts chicken stock

5 black peppercorns

2 tablespoons flat-leaf parsley, chopped

Kosher salt and freshly ground black pepper

1 pound mini ricotta ravioli

Parmigiano-Reggiano cheese

Shred meat from carcass of the chicken and set aside. In a large pot over medium heat, add celery, carrots, onion, thyme, chicken stock, peppercorns, parsley, salt, and pepper. Bring to a boil, and simmer for one hour.

In a second pot, boil water for the mini ravioli. When water begins to boil, add salt liberally. Let water return to a boil. Add mini ravioli, and cook until al dente. Drain and add to soup along with the shredded chicken. Top with Parmigiano-Reggiano and more parsley when serving.

White Bean and Escarole Soup

When I was a little girl, I disliked escarole intensely. My mother would prepare it in various ways, hoping to entice me, but I refused to eat it. Finally, when I became an adult, I learned to appreciate this fine vegetable, most especially in soups with pure, rustic ingredients. My escarole-and-bean soup is best served with a loaf of warm, crusty bread.

1/2 pound dried white cannellini beans

1 tablespoon extra-virgin olive oil

1 large onion, chopped

2 carrots, chopped

2 celery stalks, chopped

3 garlic cloves, peeled and crushed

2 cups escarole, roughly chopped

2 quarts vegetable or chicken stock

1/2 teaspoon crushed red pepper flakes

1 14.5-ounce can diced tomatoes

Kosher salt and freshly ground black pepper

Parmigiano-Reggiano cheese, freshly shaved

In a bowl, cover the beans with water and refrigerate overnight. Drain well. Heat the oil in a large pot over medium-high heat. Add the onion, carrots, and celery and sauté until tender, about five minutes, stirring occasionally. Add the garlic and cook over low heat for two more minutes. Add the drained beans, escarole, stock, red pepper flakes, tomatoes, salt, and pepper. Simmer for forty minutes. Top with shaved Parmigiano-Reggiano when serving.

Sweet-and-Sour Soup

When I am in an adventurous mood (which is most of the time!), I enjoy delving into Asian cuisine. After reading many Chinese and Japanese cookbooks, and experimenting in the kitchen, I came up with my own variation of sweet-and-sour soup.

1/4 cup Chinese black dried mushrooms

2/3 cup water

2 tablespoons tapioca starch

4 ounces lean pork, cut into fine strips

1 tablespoon sherry

2 quarts chicken stock

1/4 cup bamboo shoots, sliced into thin strips

1/2 cup tofu, diced

2 tablespoons soy sauce

2 tablespoons white rice vinegar

1 teaspoon sesame oil

Salt and white pepper, to taste

1 egg, beaten

2 scallions, chopped

Soak mushrooms in warm water for thirty minutes. Drain, reserving the water. Remove stems and discard. Slice the caps. Mix the tapioca starch into the mushroom water, forming a paste.

Soak the pork strips in the dry sherry for ten minutes. In a large pot, combine chicken stock, pork strips, bamboo shoots, and mushrooms. Add tapioca paste to soup, and mix thoroughly. Allow tapioca starch to thicken soup, and then simmer for thirty minutes.

Add tofu, soy sauce, white rice vinegar, sesame oil, and pepper. Simmer for fifteen minutes. Turn the heat off. Drizzle the beaten egg from fingertips, while stirring the soup in the same direction, so that it creates threads of egg. Serve with a garnish of scallions.

Camille's Tip: There is more than one type of tofu, silky, soft, firm, and extra firm. For this recipe, it is best to use firm so that the tofu will maintain the cubed shape.

Shrimp-and-Scallop Soup

I cook huge seafood dinner, and, in the past, I would offer rich and tasty seafood offerings on my catering menu. However, I would rarely include a soup. I realized it was time to serve one, and included two of my favorite seafoods, shrimp and scallops, when I created this recipe.

1 tablespoon olive oil

4 garlic cloves, peeled and crushed

1/8 teaspoon red pepper flakes

1/2 cup tomato paste

2 quarts fish stock

1 tablespoon Old Bay Seasoning

1 teaspoon dill

2 tablespoons rosemary

2 cups clam juice

Kosher salt and freshly ground black pepper

1/4 cup butter

1/2 cup dry white wine

1 pound medium shrimp, peeled and de-veined

1 pound bay scallops

Fresh flat-leaf parsley, for garnish

In a large pot, warm olive oil over medium heat. Add garlic, and cook until tender. Add red pepper, and cook until sizzling. Stir in tomato paste, and cook ingredients together, allowing flavors to combine. Add fish stock, Old Bay Seasoning, dill, rosemary, clam juice, salt, pepper, and butter. Bring to a fast boil for a few minutes, reduce heat to low, and simmer one hour. Add wine to the soup, and continue to simmer for fifteen minutes. Add shrimp and scallops, and simmer until scallops and shrimps are fully cooked. Garnish with parsley.

Pasta

When I was a little girl, it was the ritual in my parents' Italian American home to prepare a pasta feast every Sunday. As pasta is at the cooking heart of most Italian homes, my mother made a different but traditional one every weekend. On Sunday afternoon, our family would gather around my mother's long dining room table. Guests were invited very often. We would find ourselves in front of warm aromatic bowls of any pasta from piping lasagna oozing with fresh ricotta and melted mozzarella, to potato gnocchi topped with a rich red sauce and fresh green basil. As the years

 *went by and I became more deeply engrossed in all things culinary, I grew more and more in my knowledge of pasta and my sheer love of its versatility. Whatever your taste buds crave, be it veggies, cheeses, meats, or fish, be creative and daring. Add glorious fresh herbs and zesty spices and pair it all up with an al dente pasta. In most cases, you will*

have a very worthy meal. For the following recipes, I suggest serving the pasta in a family-style platter or in warmed individual bowls.

Camille's Marinara Sauce

A truly delicious marinara sauce that is packed with incredible flavor is something people will never forget upon that first taste. My method in preparing marinara is slightly different from other experienced cooks and chefs, and it yields outstanding results.

I have taught the preparation of this sauce in my culinary class countless times and to all age groups. I begin by teaching my students the origins of this Southern Italian sauce. Legend tells us that it was prepared by Neapolitan sailors when they came into port and wanted an uncomplicated meal. In our day and age, it has become the foundation for a great deal of Italian cooking, and you can even take this sauce a step further by adding seafood, pork or beef. Marinara sauce is also ideal for rice dishes and pizza.

10 garlic cloves, peeled
20 fresh basil leaves
1/4 cup extra virgin olive oil, plus more
1/8 teaspoon red pepper flakes
1 small onion, chopped
Kosher salt and freshly ground black pepper
2 28 ounce cans crushed tomatoes (I prefer Tutta Rosa)
Parmigiano-Reggiano cheese, grated

Place garlic and basil in a food processor and stream in the olive oil as ingredients pulse. In a sauce pot, warm additional olive oil over medium heat, just enough to cover the bottom. Add the red pepper flakes, and allow the flakes to sizzle slightly and flavor the oil. Add the onion and cook until tender. Spoon the garlic and basil mixture into the sauce pot. Season with a generous amount of salt and pepper. Stir constantly for about five minutes as the ingredients come together and the fragrances release. Pour in crushed tomatoes. Stir the ingredients together very well and add more salt and pepper to taste. Raise heat high for just a few minutes, and then lower heat to simmer, covered, for one hour.

In a large pot, boil water for your pasta of choice. When water begins to boil, add salt liberally. Let water return to a boil, and cook pasta until al dente. Drain the pasta and return it back to the pot. Add a generous amount of marinara and toss well. When serving, sprinkle with Parmigiano-Reggiano cheese and garnish with fresh basil.

Pappardelle with Walnut and Sage Sauce

My mother rarely cooked with sage, but I find the slightly bitter leaves, with such a pungent flavor, to work well in many recipes, including poultry, pork, and veal. You can find fresh sage in the herb section of your supermarket.

2 tablespoons butter

1/4 cup walnuts, chopped

1 shallot, chopped

2 tablespoons fresh sage

1/2 cup dry white wine

2/3 cup heavy cream

1/2 pound pappardelle

Parmigiano-Reggiano cheese, grated

In a large pot, boil water for the pappardelle. When water begins to boil, add salt liberally. Let water return to a boil, and cook pappardelle until al dente. Reserve a cup of the pasta water and set aside. In a large sauté pan, warm butter over medium heat. Add walnuts and cook until toasty. Add shallots and sage and cook until shallots are tender. Stir in wine and heavy cream. On high heat, whisk for a few minutes until boiling. Lower heat, and drain the pappardelle. Add the pasta to the sauté pan. Toss ingredients together and add the reserved pasta water, as needed. Sprinkle with Parmigiano-Reggiano cheese.

Camille's Tip: Unless specifically called for, it is best to never chop sage in a recipe, as it will yield a very strong flavor. Allow the leaves to stay whole.

Spaghetti Bolognese

The key element to making a good Bolognese is patience. Browning the ingredients is important, and allowing the flavors to combine and cook together will yield a robust flavor to your pasta dish.

1/4 cup extra-virgin olive oil
1 medium onion, chopped fine
1 carrot, chopped fine
2 celery stalks, chopped fine
3 garlic cloves, peeled and chopped
Kosher salt and freshly ground black pepper
1 pound ground beef
1 pound ground pork
1/2 cup pancetta, finely diced
1 teaspoon nutmeg
1/2 cup tomato paste
1/2 cup red wine
Beef stock
Water
Parmigiano-Reggiano cheese, grated
1/2 cup fresh flat-leaf parsley, chopped

In a large sauté pan, warm olive oil over medium heat. Add onion, carrot, celery, and garlic, and cook until vegetables are tender. Season with salt and pepper. Mix in ground beef, pork, and pancetta, and brown very well while stirring. Sprinkle in nutmeg. Stir in tomato paste and red wine, and simmer over medium-low heat for one and a half hours. Add beef stock and water, taking turns, as needed when sauce thickens too much. Season more to taste with salt and pepper.

In a large pot, boil water for the spaghetti. When water begins to boil, add salt liberally. Let water return to a boil, and cook spaghetti until al dente. Drain the spaghetti and add to sauté pan, tossing well with the Bolognese. Sprinkle with Parmigiano-Reggiano cheese and garnish with fresh parsley.

Gnocchi with Maple Gorgonzola Sauce

Gnocchi is a dumpling-like pasta. When I was a little girl, my mother and my grandma Sue would serve home-made gnocchi often. I have a vivid memory of immaculate white tablecloths laid out carefully on my parents' bed. The bed was the only place big enough for the large amount of gnocchi prepared. Grandma Sue would layer the fresh pasta on the tablecloths in readiness to be boiled.

Gnocchi is known as a very filling pasta due to potatoes as an ingredient in the dough, and my addition of a creamy maple gorgonzola sauce makes this an extra rich dish. Due to this fact, I usually serve this particular pasta in smaller portions as an hors d'oeuvre rather than a major course for a dinner party. I like to add a few gnocchi bathed in the sauce into an hors d'oeuvre shot glass or a mini cocktail glass. The glasses sit attractively on a tray to be passed around to guests. While making fresh gnocchi is an adventure, it is fine to purchase a high quality brand from the freezer section of your grocer.

3 cups heavy cream

1/2 cup Gorgonzola cheese

1/3 cup maple syrup

1/4 cup tablespoons Pecorino Romano, grated

2 pounds gnocchi

Kosher salt

Fresh chives, chopped

In a medium pot, bring heavy cream to a boil. Lower to medium-low heat and allow to cook for 35 minutes while whisking occasionally. Take heavy cream off the heat and stir in gorgonzola cheese and maple syrup. Sprinkle in Pecorino Romano. In a large pot, boil water for the gnocchi. When water begins to boil, add salt liberally. Let water return to a boil, and cook gnocchi until they rise to the top. Drain well and return to the pot. Mix the maple gorgonzola sauce in until the gnocchi is well coated. Serve with a garnish of fresh chives.

Creamy Mascarpone Gemelli

I encourage the use of mascarpone cheese in many recipes. At first taste, I instantly fell for this cheese, and I enjoy adding it to my pasta. This recipe is a very simple gemelli tossed with mascarpone, marinara sauce and a lot of grated cheese. Gemelli is a spiral shaped pasta, and it will hold this creamy sauce very well.

1 pound gemelli

2 cups marinara sauce (page 227)

1/2 cup mascarpone cheese

1 cup of Parmigiano-Reggiano cheese, grated

2 tablespoons fresh flat-leaf parsley, chopped

In a large pot, boil water for the gemelli. When water begins to boil, add salt liberally. Let water return to a boil, and cook gemelli until al dente. Drain well, and pour gemelli back into the pot. Add marinara sauce, mascarpone and Parmigiano-Reggiano cheese. Garnish with parsley.

Fresh Manicotti

I have been making manicotti with my mother and my grandma Sue since childhood. It is easy to buy a box of prepared manicotti from the frozen section of the supermarket, but making it fresh is like a party in your mouth. The creamy ricotta filling encased in the firm shell, shiny with the hint of fresh eggs, is incomparable in taste.

1 cup flour, sifted

4 eggs

1 cup water

2 teaspoons kosher salt

Vegetable oil

3 cups ricotta, drained

2 cups fresh mozzarella, shredded

1 cup Pecorino Romano cheese, grated

1/2 cup fresh flat-leaf parsley, chopped

2 garlic cloves, pressed through a garlic crusher

Marinara Sauce (pg. 227)

In a blender, mix flour, eggs, water, and salt to create a batter. Warm vegetable oil in a sauté pan over medium heat. Spoon three tablespoons of batter onto the pan and carefully tilt it in a circular motion until the batter forms a round, thin layer similar to a crepe. Cook for one minute, and carefully flip the shell over with a spatula. Cook for an additional thirty seconds. Repeat process with remaining batter, and stack the cooked shells between waxed paper.

In a large bowl, mix ricotta, mozzarella, Pecorino Romano, parsley, and garlic. Spoon two heaping tablespoons into the center of a manicotti shell. Roll the shell. Repeat with remaining shells and filling.

Spoon marinara sauce evenly onto the bottom of a baking dish or pan. Arrange manicotti in the baking dish and cover with more sauce. Sprinkle with Pecorino Romano cheese. Bake in a preheated oven at 350°F for thirty minutes.

Camille's Tip: You can prepare mini manicotti for a buffet party. Make the shells in smaller rounds and use half the amount of ricotta filling.

Linguine with Cremini Mushrooms and Arugula

Arugula and mushrooms are so earthy and work very well together in this pasta dish. I like to use creminis, but any type of mushroom will work well.

1 tablespoon extra-virgin olive oil

1/8 teaspoon crushed red pepper flakes

1 cup cremini mushrooms, sliced

3 garlic cloves, peeled and chopped

1/2 cup dry white wine

1 heaping tablespoon butter

1 cup vegetable stock

1 pound linguine

1 cup packed arugula

1/2 cup Parmigiano-Reggiano cheese, grated

Truffle oil

Fresh flat-leaf parsley, chopped

In a large pot, boil water for the linguine. When water begins to boil, add salt liberally. Let water return to a boil, and cook linguine to al dente. While pasta is cooking, in a large sauté pan, warm olive oil. Add the red pepper flakes, and allow the flakes to sizzle slightly and flavor the oil. Stir in mushrooms and garlic and cook until tender. Stir in wine, and allow it to reduce by half. Mix in butter and vegetable stock. Drain the linguine, and add it to the sauté pan. Add arugula, tossing the ingredients well. Sprinkle with Parmigiano-Reggiano cheese and drizzle with truffle oil. Garnish with parsley.

Cavatelli and Cauliflower

My aunt Pauline passed this recipe down to me. She made it very often in her home, and within minutes, the huge bowl on her dining room table would be finished by her nieces and nephews.

1 head fresh cauliflower

1 tablespoon extra-virgin olive oil

1 shallot, diced

1 28-ounce can crushed tomatoes

1/2 cup fresh flat-leaf parsley, chopped

1/8 teaspoon crushed red pepper flakes

Kosher salt and freshly ground black pepper

1 pound cavatelli

1 cup Pecorino-Romano cheese, grated

Separate cauliflower into flowerets. Steam until tender but still firm. Plunge cauliflower into a bowl of ice water for about two minutes. Take out of water, drain very well, and pat dry. Heat the olive oil in a large sauté pan, and add shallots. Allow shallots to cook until tender. Stir in crushed tomatoes, parsley, red pepper flakes, salt, and pepper. Simmer for thirty minutes.

Cook the cavatelli in boiling water, according to package directions. Drain the cavatelli, and add it to the pan of tomato sauce. Add cauliflower and Pecorino-Romano cheese. Gently toss the ingredients well. Garnish with fresh parsley.

Camille's Tip: When steaming or boiling cauliflower, add a tablespoon of milk to the water. This will allow the white color to remain.

Bucatini with Baby Eggplants

One spring season, I was preparing my menu for Easter Sunday in readiness for twenty guests to share the holiday together in my home. When shopping in a gourmet market in Bensonhurst, Brooklyn, an area very heavily populated with Italian Americans, I came across a mountain of shiny purple baby eggplants. I knew these enchanting little vegetables had to be part of my Easter feast. In the past, I would stuff them with a tasty filling and bake them in white wine, but I yearned for a new way of preparing them.

As I approached the counter to the meat and cheese section of the market, I asked the butcher if he had a different idea on how to make baby eggplants.

Upon hearing my question, a little old Sicilian lady shopping nearby piped up with an answer. She took the eggplant out of my hand, held it up, and said with a heavy Italian accent, "Young lady, Ima gonna give you a wonderful recipe for this here melanzana!"

She then proceeded to recite a recipe of filling the eggplants with garlic, mint, and a special cheese made from sheep's milk, called caciocavallo, and then simmering them in a tomato sauce. Both the butcher and I were immediately taken with her recipe, and I thanked her profusely. The butcher behind the counter materialized an aromatic piece of the caciocavallo cheese for me to purchase and stated that he was going to tell his wife about this recipe. As for me,

I tweaked the recipe a bit by adding mint to the sauce as well, and I have been making these eggplants ever since that day. It receives raves and great appreciation!

6 baby eggplants

1 cup fresh mint

 12 garlic cloves, crushed

Large chunk of caciocavallo cheese

1/2 cup extra-virgin olive oil

1/8 teaspoon crushed red pepper flakes

1 28-ounce can crushed tomatoes

2 tablespoons fresh flat-leaf parsley

Kosher salt and freshly ground black pepper

1 pound bucatini pasta

Slice off tops of eggplants. Make three one-and-a-half-inch diagonal slits, from top to bottom, in each eggplant, evenly spaced. For each eggplant, fill one slit with a spoonful of fresh mint, the next slit with a crushed garlic clove, the third slit with a generous slice of caciocavallo cheese.

In a large sauté pan, warm the olive oil. Brown the eggplants, a few at a time, for three minutes on each side. Remove eggplants and set aside on a dish. Add the remaining crushed garlic to the sauté pan, and cook until tender. Sprinkle in the red pepper flakes, and cook until sizzling. Stir in crushed tomatoes, remaining mint, parsley, salt, and pepper. Place in the eggplants. Simmer for one hour.

In a large pot, boil water for the bucatini. When water begins to boil, add salt liberally. Let water return to a boil. Add bucatini, and cook until al dente. Drain bucatini, and serve along with baby eggplants and a generous amount of sauce. Add shaved caciocavallo cheese. Garnish with fresh parsley and fresh mint.

Linguine with Basil and Spinach Pesto

Aromatic and nutty is how I always describe pesto. Every spring, my brother plants pots of herbs and delivers them to family members. It is such a pleasure to pick the basil right off the plant when I make this earthy dish.

2 cups packed fresh basil leaves

1 cup packed fresh baby spinach

3 garlic cloves, peeled

1/3 cup pine nuts

Kosher salt and freshly ground black pepper

1 cup extra-virgin olive oil

1 pound linguine

3/4 cup freshly grated Parmigiano-Reggiano cheese, grated

Place basil, spinach, garlic, pine nuts, salt, and pepper in a food processor and stream in the olive oil as ingredients pulse. In a large pot, boil water for the linguine. When water begins to boil, add salt liberally. Let water return to a boil. Add linguine, and cook until al dente. Drain the linguine and toss with a generous amount of pesto. Add Parmigiano-Reggiano cheese.

Camille's Tip: Do not refrigerate your basil. Instead, place in a container of water and keep at room temperature.

Penne with Roasted Cherry Tomatoes and String Beans

I serve this with a nice loaf of crusty garlic bread and tall glasses of Pellegrino for a Saturday afternoon lunch.

2 cups cherry tomatoes, halved

2 cups string beans, chopped

3 garlic cloves, peeled and crushed

1 cup fresh basil, chopped

1/4 cup red onion, diced

1/2 cup extra-virgin olive oil

1 tablespoon fresh oregano

Kosher salt and freshly ground black pepper

1/8 teaspoon crushed red pepper flakes

1 pound penne

1/2 cup Parmigiano-Reggiano cheese, grated

In a bowl, toss cherry tomatoes, string beans, garlic, basil, red onion, olive oil, oregano, salt, pepper, and red pepper flakes until well coated. Layer mixture on a flat baking sheet. Bake in a preheated oven at 350°F for twenty minutes.

In a large pot, boil water for the penne. When water begins to boil, add salt liberally. Let water return to a boil, and cook penne until al dente. Reserve one cup of the pasta water. Drain penne and toss with baked cherry tomatoes mixture. Add pasta water as needed. Sprinkle in Parmigiano-Reggiano. Garnish with fresh basil.

Orecchiette with Pancetta and Peas

Orecchiette are shaped like small ears, and they are a delightful pasta to cook. I also find the pancetta and peas come together as a satisfying comfort dish. Use a spoon to scoop it up out of the bowl!

2 tablespoons extra-virgin olive oil

1/8 teaspoon red pepper flakes

1 cup pancetta, in small cubes

1 shallot, chopped

1 tablespoon chicken base

3 garlic cloves, peeled and crushed

1 cup crushed tomatoes

Kosher salt and freshly ground black pepper

1 package frozen green peas

2 tablespoons fresh flat-leaf parsley, chopped

1 pound orecchiette pasta

1 cup Parmigiano-Reggiano cheese, grated

In a large sauté pan, warm olive oil over medium heat. Sprinkle in the red pepper flakes, and allow the flakes to sizzle slightly and flavor the oil. Add pancetta and cook until browned. Stir in shallot and chicken base and cook until translucent. Add garlic and cook until tender. Mix in crushed tomatoes, salt and pepper. Simmer for fifteen minutes. Stir in frozen peas and cook for another five minutes. Add parsley.

In a large pot, boil water for the orecchiette. When water begins to boil, add salt liberally. Let water return to a boil, and cook orecchiette to al dente. Reserve a cup of the pasta water and set aside. Drain the orecchiette and add to sauté pan, tossing all ingredients well. Add reserved water, as needed. Sprinkle with Parmigiano-Reggiano cheese, and garnish with fresh parsley.

Spaghetti with Scallions

This recipe is just a twist on traditional garlic-and-oil pasta, which is a very popular quick pasta dish among Italians. I replaced the garlic with the scallions, and it yields a lightly sweet flavor.

1 pound spaghetti

2 tablespoons extra-virgin olive oil

1/8 teaspoon crushed red pepper flakes

4 whole scallions, chopped in one-inch pieces

Kosher salt and freshly ground black pepper

1/2 cup marinara sauce (page 227)

Fresh flat-leaf parsley

Ricotta salata cheese

In a large pot, boil water for the spaghetti. When water begins to boil, add salt liberally. Let water return to a boil, and cook spaghetti to al dente. In a large sauté pan, warm olive oil over medium heat. Sprinkle in the red pepper flakes, and allow the flakes to sizzle slightly and flavor the oil. Add scallions and allow to cook until fragrant. Sprinkle salt and pepper. Stir in marinara sauce and allow to simmer for three minutes. Reserve a cup of the pasta water, and drain the spaghetti. Add spaghetti and reserved water to sauté pan and toss well with scallions. When plating, add ricotta salata cheese on top. Garnish with fresh parsley.

Camille's Tip: When buying scallions, the tops should be bright green and the white ends should be firm and blemish-free.

Fettuccine and Baby Artichokes

Traditionally, Italians will stuff artichokes with a bread filling, or with garlic and parsley, and serve them as an appetizer. This recipe allows us to enjoy the unique flavor of artichokes in a tomato sauce.

12 baby artichokes

1/2 cup extra-virgin olive oil

1/2 vegetable stock

2 cups seasoned bread crumbs

1/2 pound Genoa salami, shredded

1 cup fresh mozzarella, shredded

1 cup Pecorino-Romano cheese, grated

2 tablespoons fresh flat-leaf parsley, chopped

1 egg, beaten

3 garlic cloves, peeled and chopped

2 28-ounce cans crushed tomatoes

Kosher salt and freshly ground black pepper

1/8 teaspoon crushed red pepper flakes

Wash artichokes and cut off stems at base. Mince stems and reserve. Snip off top quarter of leaves. Spread artichokes and remove fuzzy centers with a spoon in order to create a hollow. In a bowl, mix half the olive oil with vegetable stock, bread crumbs, Genoa salami, mozzarella, Pecorino-Romano cheese, and parsley. Firmly, fill the bread crumb mixture into the center of each artichoke to the top. Dip the top of each artichoke into the egg.

In a large pot, warm remaining olive oil. Brown the tops of the artichokes, turning the bread crumb side down, a few at a time. This will seal in the bread crumbs. Remove the artichokes from the pot and set aside on a dish. Add garlic and minced artichoke stems to olive oil and cook until tender. Place the artichokes standing up in the pot as the garlic and stems cook. Carefully and slowly, pour the crushed tomatoes into the pot over the artichokes. Add salt, pepper, and red pepper flakes. Simmer for one hour and fifteen minutes.

In a large pot, boil water for the fettuccine. When water begins to boil, add salt liberally. Let water return to a boil, and cook fettuccine until al dente. Drain fettuccine and plate with the artichokes. Sprinkle with Pecorino-Romano cheese. Garnish with parsley.

Radiatore with Broccoli Rabe and Shrimps

Two of my favorite foods are broccoli rabe and shrimp. They each have a distinct flavor, and they come together very well in this dish. For this recipe, use a big spoon!

1 pound radiatore pasta

2 tablespoons extra-virgin olive oil

2 tablespoons butter

1/8 teaspoon fresh red pepper flakes

3 garlic cloves, peeled and chopped

2 cups broccoli rabe, chopped

1 pound baby shrimp, peeled and deveined

1/2 cup dry white wine

Kosher salt and freshly ground black pepper

In a large pot, boil water for the radiatore. When water begins to boil, add salt liberally. Let water return to a boil. Add radiatore to boiling water and cook until al dente. Reserve a cup of the pasta water and set aside. In a large sauté pan, warm olive oil and butter on medium heat. Sprinkle in the red pepper flakes, and allow the flakes to sizzle slightly and flavor the oil. Add garlic and broccoli rabe. Lower heat, and cook until tender. Stir in baby shrimp and cook until pink. Pour in white wine, and stir ingredients until wine evaporates. Add salt and black pepper. Drain radiatore and add to sauté pan. Toss ingredients together and add the reserved pasta water, as needed.

Camille's Tip: When storing broccoli rabe in the refrigerator, place straight up, with stems in a glass of water.

Linguine with Mussels

Every single member of my family is a huge lover of mussels. When I serve this pasta dish for an occasion or holiday, I prepare a very large quantity, and I use at least five pounds of mussels. To share this recipe with you, I scaled it down to two pounds of mussels.

1 pound linguine

1/4 cup extra-virgin olive oil

2 tablespoons butter

8 garlic cloves, peeled and crushed

$1^1/_2$ cups clam juice (use a high quality bottled brand)

Kosher salt and freshly ground pepper

1/2 teaspoon crushed red pepper flakes

1/2 cup dry white wine

2 pounds mussels, scrubbed, beards removed

2 tablespoons fresh flat-leaf parsley, chopped

In a large pot, boil water for the linguine. When water begins to boil, add salt liberally. Let water return to a boil, and cook linguine to al dente. In a pot, warm olive oil and butter over medium heat. Add garlic and cook until tender. Stir in clam juice, salt, pepper, and red pepper flakes. Pour in wine and allow to evaporate. Add mussels. Cover and steam until mussels open. Drain linguine in colander and add to pot of mussels. Toss well to combine, and add fresh parsley.

Rigatoni with Saffron and Monkfish

Monkfish is also known as the poor man's lobster, as it has a taste and texture very similar to lobster meat. This means you can use monkfish as a less expensive substitute for a number of lobster dishes.

8 ounces monkfish, cubed

Kosher salt

2 tablespoons extra-virgin olive oil

1/8 teaspoon crushed red pepper flakes

4 garlic cloves, peeled and chopped

2 cups marinara sauce

1 cup white wine

Freshly ground pepper

2 teaspoons saffron threads

1 pound rigatoni

1 tablespoon fresh flat-leaf parsley, chopped

Sprinkle monkfish with a generous amount of salt. Let sit for ten minutes. In a large sauté pan, warm olive oil over medium heat. Sprinkle in the red pepper flakes, and allow the flakes to sizzle slightly and flavor the oil. Add garlic and cook until tender. Add the monkfish and cook until white, about one minute. Add marinara sauce, white wine, salt, and pepper. Simmer for fifteen minutes.

In a large pot, boil water for the rigatoni. When water begins to boil, add salt liberally. Let water return to a boil, and add saffron and rigatoni. Cook rigatoni until al dente. Drain rigatoni and add to sauté pan, tossing all ingredients well. Garnish with fresh parsley.

Camille's Tip: For this recipe, do not use a wooden spoon to stir the pasta pot. Wood will absorb the flavor of the saffron.

Pasta Shells with Pork Sauce

The flavors of pork and bacon add a very rich element to this red tomato sauce. When my sons were growing up, this was one of their favorite pasta dishes.

2 tablespoons extra-virgin olive oil

4 slices bacon, chopped

1 shallot, diced

1/4 cup fresh flat-leaf parsley, chopped

1 pound loose pork sausage filling

1 28-ounce can crushed tomatoes

1 tablespoon fresh sage

Kosher salt and freshly ground black pepper

1/8 teaspoon crushed red pepper flakes

1 pound medium pasta shells

1 cup Parmigiano-Reggiano cheese, grated

Basil

In a large sauté pan, warm olive oil over medium heat. Add bacon, shallots, and parsley, and cook until the shallots are tender. Add pork sausage filling, and stir until brown. Add crushed tomatoes, sage, salt, pepper, and red pepper flakes. Simmer for thirty minutes.

In a large pot, boil water for the pasta shells. When water begins to boil, add salt liberally. Let water return to a boil. Add pasta shells and cook until al dente. Drain pasta shells and add to sauté pan, tossing all ingredients well. Garnish with Parmigiano-Reggiano and fresh basil.

Pasta Carbonara

Pasta carbonara is almost always my pasta of choice when I see it on a menu. There is more than one way to prepare this dish. Some cooks and chefs use garlic. Others use onions. There is also more than one type of bacon that can be used, all-American smoked bacon, Italian-style bacon, which is pancetta, or even guanciale, the jowls of the of pig and very flavorful. After a long time of experimenting, I have my very set way on how to make carbonara. Guanciale yields a flavor that is simply unsurpassed. However, is it not easy to find, and I often make a special trip to a gourmet market. If you cannot find guanciale, then American bacon or pancetta will produce an appealing dish of carbonara too.

1 pound spaghetti

Kosher salt

2 tablespoons extra-virgin olive oil

1/2 pound guanciale, chopped

1 shallot, diced

1/4 cup white wine

1 large egg

Freshly ground black pepper

1 cup Parmigiano-Reggiano cheese, grated

1/4 cup fresh flat-leaf parsley, chopped

In a large pot, boil water for the spaghetti. When water begins to boil, add salt liberally. Let water return to a boil. Add spaghetti and cook until al dente. Reserve a cup of the pasta water and set aside. While pasta is boiling, in a large sauté pan, warm olive oil over medium heat. Add the guanciale and shallots, and cook until shallots are tender. Add white wine and cook until evaporated. Take the sauté pan off the heat. Drain spaghetti and add to sauté pan, tossing ingredients. Beat egg well and stir into the spaghetti. Add reserved water, as needed. Toss and add Parmigiano-Reggiano, black pepper, and parsley.

Farfalle with Chicken, Sun Dried Tomato and Pine Nuts

The sun-dried flavor of the tomatoes complements the chicken so well in this dish, and the nutty crunch of the pine nuts adds even more intense flavor. You can also substitute chicken for shrimp.

2 tablespoons extra-virgin olive oil

4 garlic cloves, peeled and chopped

2 skinless and boneless chicken breasts, about 4 ounces each, cut into cubes

1/2 cup sun-dried tomatoes, chopped

1/2 cup fresh basil, chopped

1/2 cup chicken stock

Kosher salt and freshly ground black pepper

1 pound farfalle

1/4 cup pine nuts, toasted

In a large pot, boil water for the farfalle. When water begins to boil, add salt liberally. Let water return to a boil, and cook farfalle until al dente. In a large sauté pan, warm olive oil over medium heat. Add garlic and cook until tender. Add chicken and cook about three minutes per side. Stir in sun-dried tomatoes, basil, chicken stock, salt, and pepper. Allow flavors to combine. Drain farfalle and toss into sauté pan, tossing all ingredients well. When plating, scatter toasted pine nuts on top.

Rotini with Steak Pizzaiola

My sister Lucy and her husband have been serving steak pizzaiola for years in their restaurant. This is my version of it, and it is especially helpful because you can just pop it in the oven when you are having a really busy day. Oregano complements the meat very well, and it is a huge crowd pleaser.

Beef chuck steak, cut into pieces, about 2 pounds
Kosher salt
8 garlic cloves, peeled and crushed
1 28-ounce can crushed tomatoes
1 tablespoon fresh oregano, or 1 teaspoon dried
Freshly ground black pepper
1/8 teaspoon crushed red pepper flakes
2 tablespoons olive oil

Salt beef chuck steak well about 15 minutes before you begin. In a baking dish, combine beef chuck steak, garlic, tomatoes, oregano, salt, pepper, red pepper flakes, and olive oil. Bake, uncovered, in a preheated oven at 350°F for one hour and fifteen minutes. In a large pot, boil water for the rotini. When water begins to boil, add salt liberally. Let water return to a boil, and cook rotini until al dente. Drain. Plate in a family-style platter, or
in warmed individual bowls, and top with the pizzaiola sauce and chuck steak.

Good Ol' Fashioned Spaghetti and Meatballs

I hear a lot of people say that Italian food is not just about spaghetti and meatballs. Of course, they are correct. However, I believe that such a fact has caused us to lose sight of how a dish of spaghetti and meatballs is just so charmingly delicious in its simplicity.

2 cups Italian bread, cubed

1/4 cup milk

2 pounds of ground beef

1 cup Parmigiano-Reggiano cheese, grated

4 garlic cloves cloves garlic, pressed through a garlic crusher

2 eggs

1/4 cup pine nuts

1/2 cup fresh flat-leaf parsley, minced

2 tablespoons extra-virgin olive oil

1 small onion, diced

2 28-ounce cans crushed tomatoes

1/2 cup basil, chopped

Kosher salt and freshly ground black pepper

1/8 teaspoon crushed red pepper flakes

In a bowl, soak Italian bread in milk. Squeeze out excess milk and discard. Shred bread into very small pieces and add to a large mixing bowl along with sirloin chop meat, Parmigiano-Reggiano cheese, garlic, eggs, pine nuts, and parsley. Mix all ingredients until well blended.

Roll meat into one-and-a-half-inch balls. In a large saucepot, warm olive oil on medium heat. Add onions and cook until translucent. Add meatballs in batches and brown on each side. Remove meatballs to a plate. Stir and scrape drippings in the pot, and add crushed tomatoes, basil, salt, pepper, and red pepper flakes. Return meatballs back to pot and simmer for one hour, stirring occasionally.

In a large pot, boil water for the spaghetti. When water begins to boil, add salt liberally. Let water return to a boil, and cook spaghetti until al dente. Drain. Plate in a family-style platter, or in warmed individual bowls, and top with tomato sauce and meatballs. Add extra Parmigiano-Reggiano. Garnish with fresh basil.

Camille's Tip: Ingredients for meatballs should always be chopped very fine so that meatballs will not fall apart. You may also bake your meatballs three-quarters of the way in a baking dish. Then add them to the sauce the last twenty minutes of simmering.

Mac 'n' Cheese

My love of mac 'n' cheese began in early childhood. As an adult, I have tried many recipes in many variations. This recipe is basic and great to serve to kids of all ages. I find that using a simple American cheese works really well. However, do not hesitate to reinvent your mac 'n' cheese. Experiment with other cheeses, such as Gruyère or Asiago. Get creative by adding lobster or pancetta or veggies. The possibilities are endless!

1 pound elbow pasta
1/2 cup butter
1 small onion, diced
1/2 cup flour
4 cups whole milk
1/2 teaspoon nutmeg
4 cups American cheese, grated
Bread crumbs

In a large pot, boil water for the elbows. When water begins to boil, add salt liberally. Let water return to a boil, and cook elbows until al dente. Drain well. Meanwhile, in a separate pot, warm butter over medium heat. Stir in onion and cook until tender. Mix in flour and whisk for a few moments, until it lightly browns in color. In another pot, heat the milk just until it boils and pour the boiling milk into the pot with butter, onions, and flour. Sprinkle in nutmeg. Stir well, and add American cheese. Simmer and stir until thick. Prepare a baking dish by lightly greasing the inside with butter and dusting evenly with bread crumbs. Mix melted cheese mixture with elbow pasta and pour into the baking dish. Sprinkle top lightly with bread crumbs. Bake in a pre-heated oven at 350°F for 35 minutes and until golden brown on top.

Camille's Tip: For mac 'n' cheese, it is best to purchase your cheese as a block and then grate it. This will allow for a much smoother cheese sauce.

Main Dishes

Main dishes are the focal point of most meals and dinner parties. Even if you are serving multiple courses and putting a lot of effort into your appetizers and dessert, people will generally define your meal by the main course.

"What are we having for dinner?"
"Chicken."

Unlike appetizers, salads, and pasta dishes, where we can just keep creating, I believe it is a good idea for a cook of any level to solidly master a few main dishes. Let those select dishes be your own, and learn to prepare them to mouthwatering perfection. People will remember you for your outstanding flounder with the lemon-and-caper sauce, or your flawless veal with  *Mediterranean seasonings. Then, as you go along, absolutely learn even more main dishes to add to your repertoire!*

Citrus Basil Veal Chops

Among the different types of meat, veal is a delicacy that is tender, lean, and smooth in taste, and it works well with most cooking methods. The recipe I share with you is relatively easy, and it combines aromatic basil with citrus. It is also works very well for a dinner party.

4 veal chops, each about 12 ounces and about 1 inch thick
Kosher salt and freshly ground black pepper
1/2 cup extra-virgin olive oil
1 teaspoon finely grated lemon zest
1 tablespoon of fresh-squeezed orange juice
3 gloves garlic, minced
3 tablespoons fresh basil, chopped

Season veal chops with salt and pepper and allow to sit for about 15 minutes. Combine salt, pepper, olive oil, lemon zest, orange juice, garlic and basil. Rub mixture very well into each veal chop. Marinate for two hours in the refrigerator. In a sauté pan, brown veal chops over medium heat, two minutes on each side. Transfer chops to the preheated 400°F oven for seven to ten minutes.

Camille's Tip: Never buy a head of garlic with green shoots at the top. They are bitter in taste.

Italian Veal Burgers

This is an attractive and multiflavored twist on our all-American burgers. You can serve this with a plate of cottage fries, and it will be a hit.

3 tablespoons extra-virgin olive oil

1/2 medium red onion, diced

1/2 medium red bell pepper, diced

2 garlic cloves, chopped

1/4 cup baby bell mushrooms, sliced

Kosher salt and freshly ground black pepper

1$^{1}/_{2}$ pounds ground veal

1 tablespoon fresh basil, chopped

1 tablespoon fresh flat-leaf parsley, chopped

1/8 teaspoon crushed red pepper flakes

1/2 cup Parmigiano-Reggiano cheese, grated

1/4 cup seasoned bread crumbs

1 egg

Toasted burger buns

4 slices of fresh mozzarella cheese

Arugula leaves

1 large beefsteak tomato, sliced

In a sauté pan, warm olive oil and add red onion, red bell pepper, garlic, and baby bell mushrooms. Cook over medium heat until vegetables are tender. Season with salt and pepper. Remove vegetable mixture from pan and allow to cool. Add to ground veal and mix well. Add basil, parsley, Parmigiano-Reggiano cheese, bread crumbs, and egg. Mix all ingredients and form into four patties. Chill for forty-five minutes. Add oil to same sauté pan. Cook veal patties for three minutes on each side. Serve on buns with a slice of mozzarella cheese, arugula, and beefsteak tomato.

Breast of Veal with Pancetta Stuffing

There was a sweet old man called Uncle John who would frequent my restaurant. He always asked us to serve breast of veal, and I remember him fondly when I prepare this dish. This particular cut does not yield a great amount of meat, and so the fun is really all in the stuffing.

1 3-to-4-pound breast of veal, trimmed, with pocket
Kosher salt and freshly ground black pepper
3 cups seasoned bread crumbs
3 eggs, beaten
1 cup pancetta, in small cubes
1 teaspoon garlic powder
1/8 teaspoon crushed red pepper flakes
1 cup Parmigiano-Reggiano cheese, grated
2 tablespoons fresh basil, chopped
2 tablespoons extra-virgin olive oil
1 cup chicken stock

Place veal, breastbone side down, on work surface. Season with salt and pepper. In a bowl, mix bread crumbs, eggs, pancetta, garlic powder, red pepper flakes, salt, pepper, and Parmigiano-Reggiano cheese. Fill pocket of veal breast with stuffing. (Bake any remaining stuffing in a separate dish in the oven and serve along with dinner.) Place veal in large roasting pan. Mix basil and olive oil in small bowl and rub on veal breast. In a preheated oven at 400°F, roast veal for twenty minutes. Reduce oven temperature to 350°F. Add chicken stock to the pan to use as a baste. Continue roasting veal two hours, basting every twenty minutes with chicken stock and pan drippings. Allow to settle for ten minutes before serving.

Beer Belly Skirt Steak

Skirt steak is a long and flat cut of beef. Although with a tendency toward toughness, it has good flavor. To minimize the toughness, skirt steaks can be either grilled or pan seared very quickly. To aid in tenderness and flavor, this cut of beef can also be marinated. The following recipe is a marinade that includes stout beer. My youngest son, Christopher, will often ask me to prepare this.

1 cup of beef stock

2 tablespoons stout beer

2 tablespoons extra-virgin olive oil

2 tablespoons brown sugar

2 garlic cloves, chopped

1/8 teaspoon crushed red pepper flakes

1 pound skirt steak, trimmed and cut into 4 portions

Kosher salt and freshly ground black pepper

Combine beef stock, stout beer, olive oil, brown sugar, garlic, and red pepper flakes in a flat dish. Add the skirt steak and coat well with the marinade. Allow steaks to marinate at room temperature for one hour. Remove from marinade and grill on each side for four minutes, for medium rare. Remove from grill, cover, and let rest for five minutes. Slice thinly against the grain before serving.

Camille's Tip: Do not move the steaks once they are on the grill. This will allow you to create a good sear on each side.

A Loaf of Meat

Otherwise known as meat loaf. My inspiration for this meat loaf comes from my father's mom, Grandma Josephine. When preparing her meatballs, she always added raisins and pine nuts, and that was my father's favorite. As for meat loaf, I have always been a fan of this comfort food, and I make it many different ways. However, this is my favorite version.

3 pounds ground beef

2 eggs, beaten

1 cup fresh ricotta, strained

2 cups seasoned bread crumbs

1/3 cup raisins

1/3 cup pine nuts, toasted

4 cloves garlic, pressed through a garlic crusher

1 cup Parmigiano-Reggiano cheese, grated

2 tablespoons fresh flat-leaf parsley, chopped

2 tablespoons fresh basil, chopped

1/2 teaspoon freshly ground nutmeg

Kosher salt and freshly ground black pepper

Extra-virgin olive oil

1 cup marinara sauce

In a large bowl, mix all ingredients very well. Brush a pan with olive oil. Mold the ground beef mixture into a loaf on the pan. Brush top with olive oil. Cover with foil and bake for one hour. Remove the foil and bake for another thirty minutes. Allow meatloaf to settle and then cut into slices and top with marinara sauce.

Camille's Tip: To taste test your meatloaf, take a small ball of the prepared meat mixture and give it a quick fry. This will allow you to adjust your ingredients and seasoning if needed.

Cherry Pepper Pork Chops

My aunt Pauline would prepare pork chops for my uncle Nicky with pickled cherry peppers. It was one of his favorite dishes, and the flavors matched so well. She would have all the ingredients cooking up in her big sauté pan, and the aroma would fill her kitchen. Aunt Pauline's combination of cherry peppers and pork was my inspiration when creating this dish.

4 center-cut pork chops, 3/4-inch thick
Kosher salt and freshly ground black pepper
1 pickled cherry pepper
1 cup Greek yogurt
1 cup seasoned crumbs
1 tablespoon fresh flat-leaf parsley, chopped

Season pork chops with salt and pepper. In a food processor, pulse the pickled cherry pepper until pureed. Add cherry pepper puree to the Greek yogurt and mix well. Combine bread crumbs and parsley. Dip the pork chops into the yogurt mixture and then in the bread crumb mixture, covering and patting well. Place on greased baking pan or dish. Bake in preheated 400°F oven for forty-five minutes.

Wild Butterfly Chicken

"I want there to be no peasant in my kingdom so poor that he cannot have a chicken in his pot every Sunday." ~Henry IV

King Henry had his ideas right, at least when it came to food. I am sure there are more recipes for chicken than any other ingredient or protein, and among those who love to cook, they all have a favorite chicken recipe to call their own. To add to that sentiment, yes, I have many chicken recipes, and I share this one because it is simple to prepare, but it also highlights a great technique—butter flying. When we butterfly our chicken we will yield much juicier breast meat because we are roasting the chicken flat and evenly.

To butterfly a chicken means to cut it down the middle of the cavity and spread it open. Your butcher will gladly butterfly your chicken. However, if you are adventurous, you can certainly do it yourself by following these simple steps. Begin by turning the chicken backside up. Using kitchen shears, closely cut down the side of the spiny center of the chicken, and then cut down the other side of the center. Remove the back. With a paring knife, cut along the white breastbone that resembles plastic at the bottom. Pop it out in a single piece. Then trim the extra fatty tissue on the chicken. You will now be able to spread the chicken in readiness for the following recipe.

1/2 cup vegetable oil

2 scallions, chopped

6 garlic cloves, chopped

Zest of a whole lemon

1 tablespoon onion, chopped

1 teaspoon chili powder

1 teaspoon paprika

1/2 teaspoon cumin

1/4 teaspoon ground coriander

1/8 teaspoon crushed red pepper flakes

Kosher salt and freshly ground black pepper

1 whole fryer chicken, 3 to 4 pounds, butter flied

Mix together the oil, scallions, garlic, cilantro, lemon zest, onion, chili powder, paprika, cumin, coriander, red pepper flakes, salt, and pepper. Add the chicken and coat it well with the marinade in a large, flat baking dish. Cover and let marinate overnight.

Remove the chicken from the marinade. Discard the marinade. Place the chicken flat in the roasting pan, skin side down. Roast in preheated oven at 350°F for one hour, until skin becomes crispy and golden. Turn the chicken over in between cooking time. When chicken is cooked, allow it to settle a for ten minutes before serving.

Chicken Kabobs with Spicy Apple Marinade

I like to serve my chicken kabobs with a simple tossed salad and some grilled veggies. This makes for a great summer dinner.

2 pounds boneless, skinless chicken breasts, cut into kabob pieces

1 tablespoon ground nutmeg

1 tablespoon brown sugar

1 teaspoon cinnamon

3 scallions, chopped

3/4 cup extra-virgin olive oil

3/4 cup organic apple juice

1/4 cup soy sauce

1/4 cup fresh thyme

3 garlic cloves, chopped

1/8 teaspoon crushed red pepper flakes

Kosher salt and freshly ground black pepper

Assemble chicken pieces in even amounts on skewers that were first soaked in water for thirty minutes. Mix all remaining ingredients into a marinade. Add the chicken to a large plastic sealable bag with half the marinade and refrigerate for at least four hours. On medium-high heat, grill kabobs five minutes on each side, until cooked and nicely charred.

Honey Baked Chicken with Shallots

This chicken recipe is a very easy one that yields a nice combination of sweet and savory. The honey on top adds a succulent golden crust.

Vegetable oil

8 chicken thighs, skin on

Kosher salt and freshly ground black pepper

1 tablespoon garlic powder

2 shallots, sliced

2 tablespoons thyme, chopped

1/8 teaspoon red pepper flakes

1/4 cup honey

Spread vegetable oil on bottom of baking dish and layer chicken pieces. Season generously with salt and pepper. Sprinkle garlic powder. Scatter shallots and thyme over chicken pieces. Bake, uncovered, in a preheated oven at 350°F for thirty-five minutes. In a small bowl, mix red pepper flakes and honey. Brush honey mixture onto each piece of chicken. Place chicken under broiler for an additional few minutes, until skin is toasted golden.

Oven-Top Turkey with Brie and Prosciutto

Whenever I make this in my kitchen, the ingredients and flavors come together very well, and very attractively too. Brie, a favorite cheese of mine, has a mild, pleasant flavor that matches well with the slightly salty and tender prosciutto, crisp, sweet pears, and the moist breast of turkey.

4 boneless, skinless turkey breasts

1/2 cup flour

Kosher salt and freshly ground black pepper

1 tablespoon butter

1 tablespoon, plus 2 tablespoons olive oil

1/2 pound wedge of brie

4 very thin slices prosciutto

1 Anjou pear, sliced thin

Arugula, radicchio, and endive

1 fresh lemon

Zest of a half lemon

Pound the turkey breasts very thin. Season the flour with the salt and pepper. Dredge the turkey breasts through the flour, shaking off any excess. Warm the butter and oil in a skillet. Cook turkey breasts in skillet about two minutes each side, until cooked through. Slice the brie very thin, and place a few slices on each breast. Place a lid on the skillet, and let the cheese melt slightly, about thirty seconds.

Remove and plate the turkey breasts. Top each with a slice of prosciutto and then a slice or two of pear. Coarsely chop the arugula, radicchio, and endive and place on top of prosciutto and pear. In a small bowl, squeeze the lemon and mix with the lemon zest and remaining olive oil. Splash the lemon and olive oil on top of the arugula, radicchio, and endive.

Camille's Tip: To get the most juice out of a lemon, place it in the microwave for ten seconds.

Lamb and Rice

This recipe was inspired by Grandma Sue. She always made lamb and rice for the family. It was one of my favorite dishes because the juices of the lamb flavored the rice so superbly.

1 cup raw white rice

1 large yellow onion, chopped

2 cups Pecorino Romano cheese, grated

1/2 tablespoon freshly ground black pepper

One rack of lamb shanks

Kosher salt and freshly ground black pepper

2 8-ounce cans of tomato sauce

1/2 cup fresh flat-leaf parsley, chopped

Water

Spread the rice evenly on the bottom of a thirteen-by-nine baking dish or pan. Sprinkle the onions, ground black pepper, and half the Pecorino Romano cheese evenly over the rice. Cut the lamb shanks into rib pieces and season with salt and pepper. Place each rib over the rice mixture, spreading them out in a row. Evenly pour the tomato sauce over the contents of the baking dish. Sprinkle remaining Pecorino Romano and the parsley. Fill the baking dish , three-quarters to the top, with water. All the ingredients will appear to swim in the dish. Place in a preheated oven at 375°F. Bake until the water disappears, the rice is fluffy, and the lamb is fully cooked.

Irish Stew

Lamb is the primary ingredient of an authentic Irish stew, and I have always found this dish to be so perfectly hearty for a cold winter night. Over the years, more than one of my Irish American friends shared their interpretation of this age-old crowd pleaser. As I experimented with it, I realized that the beauty of Irish stew is its simplicity, minus any added flourish of a roux, heavy cream, or wine.

3 pounds boneless lamb shoulder, cut into $1^1/_2$-inch pieces
2 quarts beef stock
4 red potatoes, peeled and cubed
2 large yellow onions, sliced
3 carrots, peeled and thickly sliced
3 celery stalks, thickly sliced
1 tablespoon fresh rosemary, chopped
1 tablespoon fresh thyme, chopped
Kosher salt and freshly ground black pepper
1 tablespoon fresh flat-leaf parsley

In a large pot over medium heat, combine lamb and beef stock. Bring to a boil. When foam rises to the top, skim off with a spoon. Simmer on a low flame for thirty minutes. Add remaining ingredients and simmer for about one hour or until lamb and vegetables are tender. Serve piping hot in warmed bowls, garnished with fresh parsley.

Camille's Tip: Serve this stew with a mug of Guinness, brown soda bread, and butter, and people will understand why this dish is at the top of the list of comfort foods.

Pineapple Rum-Glazed Salmon

For me, a favorite facet of salmon is the deep coral color. How enticing a perfectly prepared piece of salmon looks when plated with bright, crisp garnish or a special sauce. Salmon can be made in various different ways, including poached, smoked, or grilled. You may also marinate this special fish. The following recipe is one of my favorite ways of serving salmon. My inspiration in creating this dish was my first trip to Hawaii when I was a teen. For me, it sparked an instant love of macadamia nuts.

1/2 cup honey

1/2 cup pineapple juice

2 tablespoons rum

6 skinless salmon filets, about 5 ounces each

1/3 cup chopped macadamia nuts

Kosher salt and freshly ground black pepper

Preheat broiler. In a saucepan, cook honey, pineapple juice, and rum, uncovered and over medium-low heat, to create a glaze. Lightly grease a baking dish or pan. Place salmon filets on pan and season with salt and pepper. Broil salmon for about four minutes. Lightly brush each filet with a small amount of the glaze. Turn salmon over and broil until flaky. Do not overcook. Add chopped macadamia nuts to the pineapple-rum glaze and heat further, for about two more minutes. Drizzle nuts and remaining glaze generously over salmon and serve.

Coconut Shrimp and Apricot Dip

During my time as a restaurant owner, we would host Hawaii night. The entire staff would wear hula skirts and leis, and our menu was a festive array of Hawaiian appetizers and entrées. One of the greatest people to work with me was my dear friend Johnny. In the kitchen, Johnny and I would prepare coconut shrimp while the rest of our kitchen staff prepared everything else. It was Johnny's idea to soak the shrimp in coconut milk. He and I gave careful attention to the shrimp, as so many of our customers looked forward to ordering it. The Hawaii evenings are a thing of the past, but I still prepare this festive dish in my home.

2 pounds jumbo shrimp, peeled and deveined, with tails left on
2 cups, plus 1/2 cup coconut milk
3 eggs
2 cups panko bread crumbs
2 cups coconut flakes
Kosher salt and freshly ground black pepper
1 cup flour
Vegetable oil, for frying

In a bowl, combine shrimp with two cups of the coconut milk, making sure that shrimp is well covered. Chill for one hour. In a shallow baking dish, whisk remaining coconut milk with eggs. In a separate shallow baking dish, mix panko bread crumbs and coconut flakes Sprinkle salt and pepper in flour. Dredge shrimp in flour, then coconut milk–egg mixture, then panko-coconut mixture. Shake off excess between each dredging. In sauté pan , warm vegetable oil over medium heat. Fry shrimps in batches, without overcrowding, until golden. Serve warm with apricot dip.

Apricot Dip

1 tablespoon canola oil

2 scallions, sliced thin

Pinch of red pepper flakes

2 tablespoons soy sauce

2 cups apricot preserves

Heat the canola oil in a small saucepan. Add scallions and red pepper flakes. Allow to cook for a few minutes, until sizzling. Add soy sauce and apricot preserves. Allow to simmer for ten minutes. Serve warm with the coconut shrimp.

Camille's Tip: This recipe also goes very well with chicken in place of the shrimp. Just cut chicken breast into finger slices or medallions.

Baked Red Snapper

I have been cooking simple pieces of filet like this for years. This recipe is for red snapper, but you can prepare with any filet of your choice.

4 snapper filets, about 4 ounces each
Kosher salt and freshly ground black pepper
1 garlic clove, chopped
2 tablespoons extra-virgin olive oil
1 tablespoon dry white wine
2 tablespoons fresh-squeezed lemon juice
1/8 teaspoon crushed red pepper flakes
1 tablespoon butter
1/2 tablespoon fresh flat-leaf parsley, chopped

Season filets with salt and pepper. Place in a baking dish or pan and add garlic. Whisk olive oil, wine, lemon juice, and red pepper flakes. Pour mixture over filets. Dot with butter, and sprinkle with parsley. Bake in preheated oven at 450°F for twenty minutes.

Camille's Tip: When defrosting fish, thaw it in milk. This will yield a fresh-caught taste and appearance. Discard the milk after the fish thaws.

Swordfish with Sun-Dried Tomato and Artichokes

The combination of sun-dried tomatoes and artichokes add color and great taste when combined in a recipe, and the swordfish holds very well with these two favored ingredients.

2 swordfish filets, 5 ounces each

Kosher salt and freshly ground black pepper

4 sun-dried tomatoes, coarsely chopped

1/2 cup baby artichokes, quartered

1/4 cup Gaeta olives

2 garlic cloves, chopped

1 tablespoon fresh basil, chopped

1 tablespoon fresh flat-leaf parsley, chopped

2 tablespoon extra virgin olive oil

Season the swordfish with salt and pepper, and place each filet on a large piece of aluminum foil. In a bowl, mix sun-dried tomatoes, artichokes, olives, garlic, basil, parsley, olive oil, salt, and pepper, and toss together. Add the sun-dried tomato and artichoke mixture evenly on top of each swordfish filet. Tent the sides of the aluminum foil up into a pouch and close securely. Place the pouches on a baking sheet and bake in preheated oven at 400°F for twenty minutes.

Cut open aluminum pouch and remove swordfish. Place on warm plates, and serve with extra garnish of basil and parsley.

Camille's Tip: You may use frozen artichoke hearts for this recipe. Be sure to defrost them first.

Cheese Soufflé

In the past few years, I decided that I was finally going to bake a knockout soufflé. After reading a lot of material, I must admit that I was a bit intimidated. But, of course, that was not going to stop me. Admittedly, my first few times were not successful. But after some practice, I finally put together a few rules that aid toward creating this dish. First, the egg whites must never have egg yolk still lingering in them once the eggs are separated. Even a very small bit of yolk will prevent the whites from forming into peaks because the fat content of the yolks will hinder the air performance in the whites. Next, always bake the soufflé on the bottom of the oven and not the middle of the oven, as in most recipes. We do this because it is the direction of the heat, rising from down to up, that causes the soufflé to rise. We also never open the oven door for at least the first fifteen minutes of baking. Finally, always use a dish specially made for a soufflé of metal, timbale, or porcelain, and always make sure it is fully and generously greased with butter.

There are countless recipes out there for soufflé. Many are made vegetarian, or with seafood, or with fruit. But for me, I am a big fan of the classic cheese soufflé.

Butter for greasing, plus 2 ½ tablespoons
Grated cheese of choice
3 tablespoons flour

1 ¼ cups milk

4 eggs, separated, plus one egg white

1/2 teaspoon cayenne pepper

3/4 cup cheddar cheese

1 tablespoon chives, chopped

1/4 teaspoon cream of tartar

Grease the inside of a medium-sized soufflé dish and dust with grated cheese. In a small pot, warm remaining butter over medium heat. Mix in flour and whisk for a few moments (do not brown). Pour in milk, and allow to come to a full boil. Remove from heat. Whisk the egg yolks and cayenne pepper. Slowly stir the yolks into the milk, a bit at a time. Add the cheddar cheese and chives. Beat the five egg whites and cream of tartar until peaks form. Fold in egg whites to yolk mixture and transfer to the prepared baking dish. Bake at 350°F for 30 minutes, until puffed and golden.

Vegetables and Sides

Our vegetables add the rainbow of colors to our food. To me, they are akin to the accessories to an outfit or the flowing curtains and décor to a room, adding another dimension of value to a meal in order to make it complete.

When it comes to our vegetables, blanching and shocking is a cooking method that should be used often. The idea is to serve crisp and tender vegetables minus a mushy finish. To blanch and shock, boil a pot of water. On the side, prepare a bowl of very cold water filled with ice. Place your vegetables, a few at a time, into the boiling water. Do not overcrowd. Boil the vegetables for about a minute or so, depending on thickness. Test the vegetables for  *doneness by inserting a knife for tenderness. When the vegetables are done, remove them from the boiling water and plunge them into the ice bath to begin the "shocking" process. The cooking will now stop. Cool the vegetables completely, and then drain them well on paper towels before adding salt or other seasoning.*

Swiss Chard Fritters

This is my favorite way to serve Swiss chard. The fritters are just scrumptious by themselves, or with a dusting of grated cheese. I also include a caper sauce, which is great if you are preparing these fritters as a pass-around appetizer for guests.

1 large bunch of fresh Swiss chard
2 eggs
1/2 cup Bisquick
Kosher salt and freshly ground black pepper
Vegetable oil
Parmigiano-Reggiano cheese (optional)

Rinse Swiss chard thoroughly. Chop, and boil until tender. Squeeze out excess water very well. Mix Swiss chard with eggs, Bisquick, salt, and pepper. In a sauté pan, warm vegetable oil until hot and gently drop in generous spoonfuls of the Swiss chard mixture. Fry on each side a few minutes, until golden. Sprinkle with Parmigiano-Reggiano cheese and serve warm, or serve with caper dipping sauce.

Caper Dipping Sauce
1/2 cup mayonnaise
1/2 cup sour cream
1 tablespoon capers, rinsed, drained and patted dry
1 scallion, chopped

Dash of Tabasco Sauce

Zest of one lemon

Kosher salt and freshly ground black pepper

Mix all ingredients well.

Camille's Tip: You may prepare this recipe with spinach or asparagus also. Just steam and chop the vegetables until tender, and proceed with the recipe as described.

Buttermilk Cauliflower

This recipe encloses the cauliflower in a fluffy and crisp batter. I usually serve this on Thanksgiving. It also is a great addition to Easter Sunday dinner.

1 head of fresh cauliflower

3 large eggs

1/2 cup buttermilk

1/2 cup Bisquick

1/2 teaspoon cayenne pepper

Kosher salt and freshly ground black pepper

2 tablespoons chopped parsley

Vegetable oil

Cut and separate raw cauliflower into florets. Boil until tender but still firm. Plunge cauliflower into a bowl of ice water for about two minutes. Take out of water, drain very well, and pat dry. Whisk eggs, buttermilk, Bisquick, cayenne pepper, salt, pepper, and chopped parsley to create a batter (should be lighter than a pancake batter) coat each piece of cauliflower well. In a sauté pan, warm vegetable oil over medium heat. Fry each floret, turning occasionally, until golden, a few minutes each side. Sprinkle each floret with additional salt.

Broccolini with Olives and Pine Nuts

Broccolini is a cousin to the better known broccoli and one of my favorite vegetables. The stalks are slimmer and longer, and the florets are smaller. In this recipe, the olives give a nice balance to the crunch of the pine nuts, and the lemon juice adds a zesty tartness when biting into the broccolini.

2 bunches broccolini

1/2 cup black pitted olives, sliced

1/4 cup pine nuts

2 tablespoons fresh-squeezed lemon juice

2 tablespoons white vinegar

1/3 cup extra-virgin olive oil

2 garlic cloves, chopped

Kosher salt and freshly ground black pepper

Cut broccolini into florets and discard stems. Steam or boil until tender but still firm. Plunge broccolini into a bowl of ice water for about two minutes. Take out of water, drain very well, and pat dry. Chill for one hour. In a bowl, gently mix broccolini, olives, and pine nuts. In another bowl, mix lemon juice, white vinegar, olive oil, garlic, salt, and pepper. Add the dressing to broccolini and coat well, turning gently.

Camille's Tip: You may cook the broccolini a few hours before and chill it in the fridge before preparing this recipe.

Parmesan Spaghetti Squash

Cooking spaghetti squash with these ingredients is just pure and simple flavor. Serve it piping hot.

2 large spaghetti squash, halved and cleaned
1/2 cup extra-virgin olive oil
Kosher salt and freshly ground black pepper
2 tablespoons basil, chopped
1/2 cup Parmigiano-Reggiano cheese, grated

Place spaghetti squash in a baking dish and brush generously with half of the olive oil. Season with salt and pepper. Bake in a preheated oven at 375°F for fifty minutes until skin is soft. Remove squash from oven and cool slightly, to handle. Remove the inside of the squash to a bowl and mix with basil, Parmigiano- Reggiano cheese and remaining olive oil.

Festive Escarole

One Easter season, I was looking for a different twist on serving escarole. One of my coworkers told me that she likes to toss it with pine nuts, olives, capers, raisins, and anchovies and then stuff it into a pastry pie or pizza dough. I loved the idea of these ingredients and how the sweet and savory flavors make such a great addition to the freshness of the escarole. I tried it the first time baked into a pie, but liked the filling so much that now I just prepare the escarole with these select ingredients and serve it minus the pastry or dough addition.

2 tablespoons vegetable oil
1 tablespoon pine nuts
3 garlic cloves, chopped
1 tablespoon black olives, sliced
1 tablespoon capers, washed, drained, and patted dry
1 tablespoon white raisins
4 anchovy fillets cut in half, along with some of its oil from the jar
2 cups escarole, blanched and chopped

In a sauté pan, warm the vegetable oil on medium heat. Add pine nuts and allow to cook until toasty brown. Add the garlic, olives, capers, and raisins. Stir to allow flavors to blend. Add anchovy fillets, and allow them to cook in the mixture for a one minute, but without dissolving. Add escarole and mix very well for one minute to blend the combine the ingredients and flavors.

Camille's Tip: Like leeks, escarole tends to carry a lot of excess dirt. Soak and rinse more than once to be sure the leaves are very clean.

Roasted Asparagus Wrapped in Prosciutto

Serve this at your next party. The fresh green color of the asparagus wrapped in the deep-rose-colored prosciutto is the signal to our eyes that this combination will be just as enticing upon our taste buds!

2 pounds fresh asparagus
Extra-virgin olive oil
Kosher salt and freshly ground black pepper
2 tablespoons butter
2 garlic cloves, chopped
1/4 cup dry white wine
1 pound imported prosciutto, sliced thin

Snap the tough white ends off the asparagus and discard, or save to add in a vegetable stock. Place the asparagus on a baking sheet. Drizzle with olive oil and toss to coat the asparagus completely. Arrange them in an even layer back on the baking sheet. Sprinkle with salt and pepper. Roast the asparagus at 375°F for fifteen minutes, until tender and crisp. In a small saucepan, melt butter and a small amount of olive oil. Add garlic and cook until tender. Add wine and allow to evaporate. Wrap three tips each of asparagus together in a slice of prosciutto. Repeat until all asparagus tips are wrapped. Drizzle butter and wine mixture onto the tips of the asparagus.

Broccoli Rabe Quiche

I never read Bruce Feirstein's book *Real Men Don't Eat Quiche*, but I love his title. I also know that most any man who likes broccoli rabe will enjoy this particular quiche. Broccoli rabe and I go back a long way. In the past, I have also used it to make hero sandwiches, homemade calzones, or just tossed over pasta. It is bitter and considered a wild broccoli, also called rapini.

My aunt Pauline would often tell me a story about my grandfather's experience with broccoli rabe when he was a young husband and father. Before my grandfather owned his own fruit and vegetable market, he worked in the giant fruit and vegetable markets of New York City. Broccoli rabe, which was not yet popular here in the United States in the early nineteen hundreds, was shipped into the markets for the first time. The boss in charge had no idea what this new vegetable was. He was ready to discard it, but my grandfather, a great cook, and very appreciative of finer ingredients, advised his boss of the values of broccoli rabe. Suffice it to say, it remained.

1 cup broccoli rabe, blanched and chopped
1/2 cup mozzarella cheese, shredded
1 nine-inch pastry pie shell
4 extra large eggs, slightly beaten
1 cup light cream
1 cup Pecorino Romano cheese

Kosher salt and white pepper, to taste

Preheat oven to 350°F. Layer broccoli rabe and mozzarella cheese in the pie shell. In medium bowl, combine remaining ingredients and mix until well blended. Carefully pour over broccoli rabe and mozzarella. Bake in center of oven for one hour until golden. Allow to settle for ten minutes before serving.

Mascarpone and Roasted Garlic Potato Bake

I have been making my potato bake since I was a teenager. My mother described my grandma Carmela's original potato pie to me, and I took it from there. The garlic is the major key to making this an exciting and flavorful way to serve a potato dish.

15 garlic cloves, unpeeled

1 tablespoon extra virgin olive oil

3 pounds Idaho potatoes, peeled and cut into even-sized cubes

1 cup Parmigiano-Reggiano cheese, grated

1/4 cup mascarpone cheese

1/3 cup milk

1/2 stick butter, plus more melted butter for topping

2 tablespoons fresh flat-leaf parsley, chopped

2 cups shredded mozzarella, plus more for topping

Kosher salt and freshly ground black pepper

Seasoned bread crumbs

In a small bowl, toss the garlic cloves with the extra virgin olive oil to coat well. Place the garlic in a piece of aluminum foil. Tent the sides of the aluminum foil up into a pouch to close securely. Place the pouch on a baking sheet and bake in a preheated oven at 350°F for thirty minutes.

Place potatoes in a pot, and add just enough cold water to cover. Bring to a boil, and lower to simmer for another ten minutes or until potatoes are tender enough for a fork to pass through. Drain the potatoes well in a colander. Return them to the pot and mash them with a potato masher. Add the baked garlic cloves, Parmigiano-Reggiano, mascarpone, milk, butter and parsley. Mix very well. Butter a baking dish or pan, and sprinkle bread crumbs to coat the inside. Spread half the potato mixture evenly in the baking dish. Add a layer of mozzarella. Spread a second layer of the remaining potato mixture. Top with more mozzarella, bread crumbs, parsley and dots of butter. Bake in preheated oven at 350°F for thirty-five minutes.

Camille's Tip: Never boil your potatoes and refrigerate them ahead of time. This will create a waxy texture.

Orange Roasted Yams

This is a recipe that my father taught me. He and I would make it along with a turkey dinner in the autumn. This recipe calls for maple syrup. As it is a bit costly, you may substitute with Karo syrup.

4 yams, peeled and cut in half diagonally

Kosher salt and freshly ground black pepper

2 tablespoons light brown sugar

2 tablespoons butter, melted

1/4 cup maple syrup

1/4 cup orange juice

The zest of a medium-size orange

Place yams, flat side down, in a baking dish. Season with salt and pepper. Bake in preheated oven at 375°F for fifteen minutes. Mix brown sugar, melted butter, maple syrup, orange juice, and orange zest. Gently pour over yams. Continue to bake another thirty minutes.

Camille's Tip: This recipe is a wonderful addition to the Thanksgiving table. You may also scatter apples and allow them to roast in the maple syrup and orange juice.

Zucchini Boats

The first time I put this recipe together, I was very pleased. I can still recall opening the oven door and enjoying the tantalizing aroma of the zucchini baking with the wine and pancetta.

4 zucchini
2 tablespoons vegetable oil
2 tablespoons shallots, chopped
2 tablespoons pancetta, chopped
2 tablespoons dry white wine
3 garlic cloves, chopped
1 cup French bread, cubed
1/2 tablespoon fresh mint, chopped
1/2 cup Parmigiano-Reggiano cheese, grated
2 tablespoons extra-virgin olive oil

Slice each zucchini in half lengthwise, and scoop out the flesh to make a hollow to create a boat. Cut off a very thin slice underneath the zucchini boat so that it will lay flat without tipping over. Chop the zucchini flesh and set aside. Parboil the zucchini boats for a few minutes. Allow to cool.

In a sauté pan, warm vegetable oil over medium heat. Add shallots and pancetta and cook until shallots are transparent. Pour in white wine and allow evaporating. Stir in garlic and chopped zucchini and continue to cook. Add the French bread cubes, mint, and Parmigiano-Reggiano cheese. Stir well over heat, allowing flavors to combine. Spoon mixture into zucchini boats and sprinkle with grated cheese. Place them in a baking dish or pan, and add white wine and olive oil to the bottom. Bake at 350°F for thirty-five minutes or until the zucchini boats are tender.

Camille's Tip: Always pick shiny and dark green zucchini. For this recipe, use the large ones, as they are starchier and better for stuffing.

Baked Carrots

This is my very simple way of serving carrots. They are so brightly healthy and colorful, and the brown sugar and syrup is just a neat way to give this favorite vegetable a nice lift.

1 pound carrots

2 tablespoon melted butter

1 tablespoon brown sugar

1/2 tablespoon garlic powder

1/2 cup maple syrup

1/8 teaspoon red pepper flakes

Kosher salt and freshly ground black pepper

2 tablespoons mint, chopped

Peel carrots, slice in half and chop into two-inch pieces. Toss carrots with remaining ingredients in a bowl. Layer carrots in a baking dish and roast in a preheated oven at 375°F for forty-five minutes. Garnish with more mint.

String Bean and Carrot Sake Toss

This is a dish I created with the addition of sake, a Japanese white wine. I like to serve this with grilled tuna steak.

1 tablespoon vegetable oil

2 teaspoons grated ginger

2 tablespoons sake

1 cup shredded carrots

2 cups string beans, chopped into one-inch pieces

1 tablespoon sugar

1 tablespoon soy sauce

1/8 teaspoon red pepper flakes

Kosher salt and freshly ground black pepper

In a sauté pan, warm vegetable oil. Add ginger, sake, carrots, string beans and sugar. Stir with a toss while allowing to cook until crisply tender, about five minutes. Add soy sauce, red pepper flakes, salt, and pepper. Serve piping hot.

Bacon Brussels Sprouts

For a long time, I did not cook Brussels sprouts because I considered them unexciting. Then I realized that I was just not exploring enough with this particular vegetable. I started to bake them wrapped in bacon, and they became an instant hit on the dinner table!

20 Brussels sprouts
3 tablespoons olive oil
2 teaspoons chicken base
Kosher salt and freshly ground black pepper
10 slices bacon

Trim the Brussels sprouts. In a bowl, whisk the olive oil, chicken base, and pepper very well. Add the Brussels sprouts, and toss to cover in the olive oil mixture. Slice each piece of bacon in half so that you have twenty shorter pieces. Wrap each Brussels sprout in a slice of bacon. Place them in a baking dish or pan and bake in a preheated oven at 375°F for thirty minutes.

Camille's Tip: Always pick firm and green Brussels sprouts. Be sure the leaves are not yellow.

Desserts

I believe it is our desserts that evoke more memories, loving moments, and warm thoughts than any other food course. So many of us can recall a cherished grandmother happily stirring a bowl of  *cake batter, or a favorite aunt rolling out the dough for her much-anticipated cookies. I am sure that, more than any other type of food, desserts are also the recipes that are handed down most from generation to generation. As our sweet tooth is always present, so we continue to bake and enjoy recipes that hail endless flavors such as rich chocolate, warm nuts, moist coconut, sweet creams, heady liqueurs, and fresh, colorful fruits.*

As we bake and taste, it is always important to remember the golden rule: baking is a science, and we must always measure the ingredients carefully according to the recipe.

Tiramisu

Over the years, I have come across so many tiramisu recipes in different variations. This is my traditional way of preparing it. I also take tiramisu in other directions, such as adding peach schnapps instead of chocolate liqueur and thin slices of peaches as an additional layer.

2 cups heavy cream
$1^{1}/_{4}$ cup sugar
1 teaspoon vanilla extract
8 ounces mascarpone cheese
2 egg whites
1/4 teaspoon cream of tartar
1 cup freshly brewed strong espresso coffee
1/4 cup coffee liqueur
30 ladyfingers
Powdered cocoa
4 ounces semisweet chocolate

Beat heavy cream with one cup of sugar until peaks form. In a separate bowl, mix vanilla and a quarter cup of sugar with mascarpone. In another bowl, beat egg whites with cream of tartar until whites are glossy and form soft peaks. Gently fold whipped cream and egg whites into mascarpone mixture. Mix espresso with the coffee liqueur. Very quickly, dip each ladyfinger in the espresso mixture and line them on the bottom of a rectangular glass dish. Layer the mascarpone and whipped cream mixture on top. Repeat with another layer of dipped ladyfingers and then another layer of the mascarpone and whipped cream mixture. Sprinkle top layer with powdered cocoa and grate the semisweet chocolate on top. Take additional ladyfingers and snap them in half. Line them around, inserting them into the cake, against the edge of the glass dish.

Almond Crescent Cookies

This light and tasty almond cookie is what easy baking is all about, and they go really well with a warm hot chocolate or a pleasant cup of tea on a winter afternoon.

1 cup butter, softened
1/2 cup sugar
2 cups flour, sifted
1 cup almonds, chopped
1 teaspoon almond extract

Mix butter and sugar until well blended. Slowly add flour while mixing. Place almonds in food processor and pulse. Add almonds and almond extract to batter. Mix well and chill the dough for two hours. Take a small ball of cookie dough and roll it into a crescent shape. Bake in a preheated oven at 350°F for 9 to 10 minutes. Transfer to wire racks and cool.

Pignoli Cookies

The classic pignoli cookie is so favored by my family and friends that I knew I had to create my own version. Although the ingredients are costly, it is among the easiest of cookies to bake. Most bakers do not add confectioners' sugar to their dough, but I find the addition to be the key element in making this cookie work better.

2 8-ounce cans almond paste

2/3 cup sugar

1/2 cup confectioners' sugar

1/2 cup flour, sifted

1 teaspoon almond extract

 4 egg whites

10 ounces pine nuts

In a food processor, pulse the almond paste until crumbly. Add the two sugars and the flour. Spoon in the almond extract. Add the egg whites one at a time, until the mixture comes together into a dough. Place the pine nuts in a dish. Wet your hands, and roll a tablespoon full of dough into a ball. Flatten slightly and press into the pine nuts. Place on a cookie sheet a few inches apart. Bake in a preheated oven at 350°F for twenty-five minutes. Transfer to wire racks and cool. Dust with a generous amount of confectioners' sugar.

Peppermint Meringue Cookies

The great thing about meringue cookies is their lightness, yet ability to satisfy. You can go in many different directions with this particular cookie. I also bake them with citrus. A word of caution for those who like to experiment: Do not add peppermint extract. This particular extract contains an oil that will ruin the process of beating your egg whites into foamy peaks.

3 egg whites
1/4 teaspoon cream of tartar
6 tablespoons sugar
A few drops of red food coloring
2 peppermint candy canes

Line cookie sheets with parchment paper. In a mixing bowl, with an electric mixer, beat egg whites until foamy. Add cream of tartar. Continue to beat at a very high speed until high peaks form. Add the red food coloring, and gradually beat in sugar until the mixture has a stiff glossy appearance. Crush the candy bars into a very small pieces. Fold half of the pieces in, and reserve the rest. Drop by heaping teaspoonfuls, one inch apart, onto the prepared cookie sheets. Sprinkle remaining crushed candy canes over the top. Bake in a preheated oven at 225°F for one hour. Turn off oven, but do not open the door. Allow the cookies to sit in the oven, undisturbed, for one hour.

Transfer to wire racks and cool. Cookies should be stored in a tightly covered container until ready to serve.

Camille's Tip: For those wishing to serve these cookies during Hanukkah, just add a few drops of blue food coloring instead of red, and purchase candy canes in blue, as they are sold in various colors now.

Ricotta Cheesecake

Cheesecake fits in every where, any time, and any place. It can be on the table for a backyard cookout or the grand finale to a formal wedding reception. With this thought, every dessert lover who enjoys baking should master at least one cheesecake recipe.

Crust:

2 cups graham cracker crumbs

6 tablespoons butter, melted

1/3 cup sugar

Filling:

3 pounds ricotta

1 $^1/_2$ cup sugar

2/3 cups flour

5 eggs

3/4 cup heavy cream

1 $^1/_2$ tablespoons vanilla

3 tablespoons lemon juice

Zest of one lemon

In a bowl, stir graham cracker crumbs, butter and sugar very well. Press mixture onto the bottom of a spring form pan.

In a bowl, mix ricotta and sugar. Gradually stir in flour. In a separate bowl, beat eggs and heavy cream. Add vanilla and lemon juice to eggs and heavy cream. Sprinkle in lemon zest. Spoon egg mixture into ricotta and stir well. Mix all ingredients until batter is smooth. Pour onto graham cracker crust in spring form pan. Bake in preheated oven at 325°F for one hour and ten minutes or until center is firm. Allow to settle, and run a butter knife around the inside edge of the spring form pan. Chill for at least three hours before serving.

White Coconut Tea Cakes

These elegant cakes, which are actually just a finer way to present cupcakes, are perfect for a special occasion luncheon, Easter Sunday brunch, and also for Mother's Day. Since my teen years, I have followed a basic white cake recipe I found in an old cookbook published before I was even born. The cookbook was published by the company that once produced Spry, a vegetable shortening that was very popular in the nineteen forties and nineteen fifties. Over the years, I took the recipe a bit further and developed it into my own coconut cake, thus keeping the refreshing white color to the theme of the cake.

2 $^1/_2$ cups cake flour

1 $^1/_2$ cups sugar

4 teaspoons baking powder

1 teaspoon salt

1/2 cup, minus 1 tablespoon water

1/2 cup, minus 1 tablespoon milk

2 teaspoons coconut extract

2/3 cup vegetable shortening

5 egg whites, unbeaten

4 ounces coconut, plus more to decorate

In a bowl, sift cake flour, sugar, baking powder, and salt. Add water, milk, and coconut extract. Add vegetable shortening. Mix on low speed for three minutes. Add egg whites and mix an additional three minutes. Stir coconut into batter. Pour batter into cupcake pans. Bake in preheated oven at 375°F for twenty to twenty-five minutes. Transfer to wire racks and cool. Decorate with white frosting of your choice, and sprinkle with coconut.

Camille's Tip: The active strength of baking soda and baking powder are important to the outcome of your baking, and it is very simple to test their activity. Mix a bit of baking soda with vinegar. If the baking soda does not bubble, then you need to restock your kitchen with a new box. You can test baking powder by using hot water instead of vinegar.

Carrot Cake

This recipe was passed down to us by a sweet and kind old lady named Mrs. Gallo. She lived in a lovely green house around the corner from us, and she was quite the decadent baker. When I was a little girl, I would run errands to the grocer for Mrs. Gallo. She would always reward me with whatever piping hot treat was emerging from the stove in her cozy kitchen. The pure and rich flavors in her carrot cake make for an extraordinarily delicious and moist dessert, and although many carrot cakes are made with cream cheese frosting, it is not needed for this one.

1 $^{1}/_{4}$ cup vegetable oil

4 eggs

1 pound organic carrots, boiled and mashed

2 cup sugar

3 cup flour

2 teaspoon baking powder

2 teaspoon baking soda

2 teaspoon cinnamon

1 cup white raisins

1 cup walnuts, chopped

In a large bowl, mix vegetable oil, eggs, carrots and sugar. In a separate bowl, sift flour, baking powder, baking soda and cinnamon. Add dry ingredients to wet ingredients. Stir until batter is smooth.

Spoon in raisins and walnuts. Pour batter into a buttered Bundt pan. Bake in a preheated oven at 375°F for fifteen minutes. Lower heat to 350 and bake for an additional 45 minutes.

Brandy Baked Fruit Salad

Fruit salad is not just for hot summer days. It can be a warm and enticing dessert during the autumn and winter too. In this recipe, the vibrant flavors of the fresh fruit bake wonderfully with the brandy.

1 apple

1 pear

1 orange

1 /2 cup seedless grapes

2 tablespoons raisins

1/2 cup pecans

2 tablespoons butter, melted

1/4 cup karo syrup

1 tablespoon sugar

2 tablespoons brandy

Slice the apple and pear into wedges. Peel skin off oranges and remove white membranes and pits. Cut grapes in half. In a bowl, mix all ingredients, and toss together. Place equal amounts onto two large pieces of aluminum foil. Tent the sides of the aluminum foil up into a pouch and close securely. Place the pouches on a baking sheet and bake in a preheated oven at 400°F for twenty minutes. Cut open and serve piping hot in warm dishes.

Chocolate Peach Mascarpone Cups

My chocolate cups are a great addition to any dessert table. This recipe calls for a smooth mascarpone filling flavored with peach schnapps, but you can add any filling and garnish of your choice.

16 ounces bittersweet chocolate, chopped

1 cup mascarpone

2 tablespoons peach schnapps

2 tablespoons sugar

Peach slices

1/2 cup almonds, slivered

Mint leaves

Melt half the chocolate in a double boiler. Stir until smooth. Line a mini cupcake pan with mini foil cups. Brush the chocolate onto the inside of the foil cups thoroughly. Chill in refrigerator about 20 minutes. Warm the remaining chocolate in the double boiler and brush cups a second time. Chill another 20 minutes. In a bowl, mix the mascarpone, peach schnapps and sugar. Remove the foil from the chocolate cups. Fill a pastry bag with the mascarpone mixture and pipe into the mini chocolate cups. Garnish the top of each cup with peach slices, almond slivers and mint.

Strawberry Sponge Cake

One year, when I was a little girl, my mom had a record number of eighteen desserts on our Thanksgiving table. Everyone present found this amusing because we were about eighteen people gathered together to celebrate the holiday. We all laughed and talked as we enjoyed a combination of pies, cakes, cookies, and puddings. As my mother's perking coffeepot filled the house with a divine aroma, the doorbell rang.

My cousin Putty said, "Whoever is at that door, I hope they do not have a dessert in their hands!"
At the door was Nicky, a friend of my cousins Louis and Frankie, and in his hand was a giant box that held a strawberry sponge cake. This recipe is one that I am especially happy to bake because it brings back such a pleasant memory of days gone by.

1 $^{1}/_{2}$ cup flour, plus 1 tablespoon
1 teaspoon baking soda
1/2 teaspoon salt
3/4 cup butter, softened
2 cups sugar
3 eggs
1/2 pound strawberries
1 tablespoon fresh-squeezed orange juice

In a bowl, sift flour, baking soda, and salt. Set aside. In a bowl, beat butter and half the sugar on low speed until blended. Beat eggs into mixture, one at a time. Slowly fold in dry ingredients to creamed ingredients. Spread the batter into a round greased cake pan. Bake in a preheated oven at 350°F for thirty minutes. Allow to cool, and remove the cake from the pan.

In a bowl, gently crush strawberries very well. Stir the strawberries, remaining sugar, and orange juice in a saucepan over low heat until the sugar is dissolved. Increase heat to high, and bring the mixture to a full boil for a few minutes while stirring constantly. Simmer for another 25 minutes until thickened. Set strawberry mixture to the side and allow to cool slightly. Gently spoon the strawberry glaze onto the sponge cake, and allow to settle into the cake. Garnish with whipped cream and mint.

Camille's Tip: Strawberries freeze very well. Handle them gently, give them a quick wash, and drain to dry. Layer them on a baking sheet so they do not clump together when they freeze. Sprinkle with sugar, and freeze overnight. Transfer them to a container the following day.

Citrus Chocolate Balls

This treat is just a different twist on traditional chocolate bourbon balls that we often see during the holidays. The original recipe that most people use calls for melted chocolate, but I find my way of using cocoa powder to work well. My addition of orange flavors also lends a refreshing lift.

$2^1/_2$ cups finely crushed vanilla wafers

1 cup confectioners' sugar

2 tablespoons cocoa powder

2 tablespoon orange zest

1 tablespoon of freshly brewed espresso coffee

1/2 cup walnuts

1/2 cup almonds

3 tablespoons corn syrup

1/4 cup orange liqueur

Sugar

Mix vanilla wafers, confectioners' sugar, cocoa powder, orange zest and espresso. Pulse the walnuts and almonds into a fine chop in the food processer and add them to the mixture. Add corn syrup and orange liqueur. Mix very well. Roll into one-inch balls and then roll in fine sugar. Store in tight container for two days before eating.

Amaretto Baked Peaches

Peaches are my favorite fruit, and I especially enjoy adding the Amaretto to this recipe. While many married couples share a glass of wine or a cup of coffee in the evening, my parents always shared a small glass of Amaretto.

2 large ripe peaches
2 tablespoons raw sugar
1/4 cup almonds, chopped
1/4 cup pecans, chopped
4 amaretto cookies, crushed
1 tablespoon Amaretto (almond liqueur)

Cut peaches in half and remove pits. Place peaches, skin side down, in a greased baking dish or pan. In a medium bowl, combine raw sugar, almonds, pecans, amaretto cookies, and almond liqueur. Fill each peach hollow with almond and nut mixture. In a preheated oven, bake at 375°F for fifteen to twenty minutes, or until topping is toasted brown. Peaches should be soft, but still hold their shape.

Camille's Tip: When choosing peaches, they should have a sweet, fragrant smell, like perfume. They should also have a downy fuzz.

Chocolate Cheese Puffs

These light and fluffy puffs are made-to-order for a grand finale to a brunch, along with a nice warm cappuccino. They are made with puff pastry, which is a really great and versatile ingredient that can be created over and over again, either savory or sweet.

1 9 $^1/_2$-inch square puff pastry, thawed
1$^1/_2$ cups ricotta cheese, strained
2 tablespoons sugar
2 tablespoons mini chocolate chips
1 egg yolk
Water

Place a sheet of thawed puff pastry on a floured work surface. Sprinkle pastry with a little more flour. With a three-inch round pastry cutter, cut out nine circles of puff pastry. In a bowl, mix ricotta, sugar, and chocolate chips. Place a heaping spoonful of ricotta mixture on each circle. Whisk together egg yolk and a tablespoon of water. Brush the egg wash along the edges of each puff pastry. Gently fold over and firmly seal the edges, forming a half-moon puff. Place puffs on prepared baking sheet lined with parchment paper. Chill baking sheet for thirty minutes. Brush tops liberally with remaining egg wash and sprinkle with a bit of sugar. In a preheated oven, bake puffs at 400°F for fifteen minutes or until golden.

Tricolor Melon Slices with Mascarpone Rum Dip

I always served this mascarpone dip, along with my gourmet cheese trays, when I catered cocktail parties, and it was always an instant hit. My suggestion is to serve it with melons, but you can use any favored array of fruit.

Watermelon

Honeydew

Cantaloupe

1 cup mascarpone cheese

1/3 cup sugar

2 tablespoons rum

Remove the rinds from the watermelon, honeydew, and cantaloupe. Cut the melons into long slices, or you can create melon balls with a scooper. Mix the mascarpone cheese, sugar, and rum in a bowl, and arrange the fruits attractively on a tray.

Camille's Tip: When picking out melons, they should feel heavier than their size.

Vanilla Ice Cream in Cantaloupe Bowls with Cherry Glaze

I mention my grandfather Luigi often in this book. A tremendous influence in many ways, he was an Italian immigrant and a dad to eight children. He was also an excellent cook. Unlike many of his Italian male relatives and friends, he loved to cook and spend time in the kitchen with his wife, my grandma Carmela. Grandpa Luigi was an orphan as a child, but he grew to love fine things, especially fine food. By the time I knew him, he was retired after a successful time as a small-business owner. An honest and hardworking man his entire life, my grandfather always wore a custom suit and custom-made shirts upon his retirement. I remember waiting by the window to see him walking up the street with his cane and carrying a bag from the grocer. The bag always contained the contents of his next food adventure. With a twinkle in his eye, my grandfather would walk into the kitchen and put on his starched white apron. I still remember the afternoon when he shared his idea of eating vanilla ice cream scooped into the inside of a hollowed-out cantaloupe. It was pure heaven. He also had fresh cherries, and he placed them right on top of the ice cream. This was my inspiration for the following dessert.

2 ripe cantaloupes
2 cups cherries, pitted and halved
1 tablespoon unsalted butter
1 tablespoon water

3 tablespoons sugar

1 teaspoon cornstarch

Zest of half a lemon

4 large scoops vanilla ice cream

Cut the cantaloupes in half and scoop out the seeds, leaving a clean hollow. Over medium heat, bring cherries, butter, water, sugar, cornstarch, and lemon zest to a boil. Lower heat, and simmer for 15 minutes or until glaze thickens. Fill each cantaloupe hollow with a scoop of vanilla ice cream. Drizzle ice cream and cantaloupe with cherry glaze.

Moving Toward the Future...

One of the greatest joys of my life is cooking for my family, especially my sons, niece, and nephews. Knowing that I am preparing the favorite dish of someone I love makes it all worthwhile. When writing these final pages, I questioned the next generation in my family and asked them to share their favorite recipe I have prepared over the years. They actually surprised me with their answers. At first, not everyone was too sure, because they each have more than one favorite. Then I started receiving a few e-mails, then a few text messages, and finally I talked to them at length.

Christina: Wagon Wheel Pasta Salad

My niece, Christina, a dedicated schoolteacher, also loves to cook. She is always willing to chop the herbs and roll out the dough. She is also my cherished friend and Godchild. Every summer, when our family and friends gather together for fun backyard cookouts, Christina always reminds me to prepare my special pasta salad.

1 pound rotelle pasta

2 cups bocconcini (small mozzarella balls)

1 cup sun-dried tomatoes, roughly chopped (use a high quality brand and reserve the oil and seasonings from the jar)

1/2 cup extra-virgin olive oil

3 garlic cloves, chopped

1/8 teaspoon crushed red pepper flakes

1 cup fresh basil, chopped

Kosher salt and freshly ground black pepper

In a large pot, boil water for the rotelle. When water begins to boil, add salt liberally. Let water return to a boil, and cook rotelle to al dente. Drain well, and allow to cool completely. In a bowl, mix rotelle and bocconcini. Add the sundried tomatoes along with reserved oil from jar. Whisk olive oil, garlic, and red pepper flakes and add to pasta mixture. Add basil. Season with salt and pepper, and toss well.

Anthony: Baked Mushroom Caps

When my nephew Anthony graduated from college and began his career, he started to take an avid interest in cooking. He would announce to one and all that it was *his* night in the kitchen and he would do the cooking. I was quite elated, to say the least! When it comes to Anthony's favorite "Aunt Camille recipe," I was asked to share my recipe for baked mushroom caps. This makes sense because for almost every holiday I host, I receive a text message from Anthony asking me to make his favorite mushroom caps.

30 large white mushrooms
3 tablespoons vegetable oil
1 shallot, chopped
3 garlic cloves, chopped
1/2 cup dry white wine
1 loaf prosciutto or lard bread (can be found in an Italian gourmet market)
2 tablespoons extra-virgin olive oil
Flat-leaf parsley

With a damp cloth, wipe mushrooms clean. Remove stems, chop, and set aside. Roughly chop prosciutto bread and place in a food processor. Pulse a few short times, until bread crumbs are coarse.

In a large sauté pan, warm vegetable oil over medium-low heat. Add shallots and cook until translucent. Stir in mushroom stems and garlic and cook until tender. Pour white wine and allow to evaporate as the flavors combine. Add the prosciutto bread crumbs to the skillet. Stir very well, incorporating ingredients and allowing bread crumbs to become lightly moist.

Transfer filling to a shallow dish and allow to cool for ten minutes. Coat a large baking sheet with half the olive oil. Spoon the filling into the mushroom caps and arrange on the baking sheet, cavity side up. Lightly drizzle remaining olive oil over each mushroom. Bake in preheated oven at 375°F for twenty-five minutes, until mushrooms are toasted golden on top. Garnish with parsley.

Camille's Tip: When buying mushrooms, be sure to check that the stems and caps are attached snugly. This ensures that the mushrooms are fresh.

Anthony Arthur: Linguine Vongole

My nephew Anthony Arthur is affectionately nicknamed Artie within our family. Artie and I share a birthday, along with my dad, on the week before Christmas. It is always a happy time when three generations share the same birthday and we can all celebrate together during the holiday season, especially when everyone is home from school. As for Artie's favorite "Aunt Camille recipe," he told me that he enjoys my linguine vongole most. As soon as I heard this, I experienced immediate guilt! Vongole is a baby clam seafood dish that I usually serve every Christmas Eve, but in the last few years, I had been replacing it with a different seafood pasta. As of this writing, Artie is a student at Providence College in Rhode Island. Suffice it to say, when he comes home to New York from school, especially at Christmastime, I will have his linguine vongole ready for him!

1 pound linguine
1/2 cup extra-virgin olive oil
1 tablespoon butter
6 garlic cloves, peeled and crushed
2 cups clam juice
Kosher salt and freshly ground black pepper
1/2 teaspoon crushed red pepper flakes
2 pounds cherrystone clams (vongole), soaked and scrubbed
1/3 cup dry white wine

1/4 cup fresh flat-leaf parsley, chopped

In a large pot, boil water for the linguine. When water begins to boil, add salt liberally. Let water return to a boil, and cook linguine to al dente. In a pot, warm olive oil and butter over medium heat. Add garlic and cook until tender. Stir in clam juice, salt, pepper, and red pepper flakes. Pour in wine and allow to evaporate. Add clams. Cover and steam until clams open. Drain linguine in colander and add to pot of clams. Toss well to combine, and add fresh parsley. Plate in a family-style platter or in warmed individual bowls. Garnish with more parsley.

Christopher: Pancetta Pasta

My youngest son Christopher told me that he had no idea what his favorite could be among all the many recipes and dishes I have cooked over the years. I told him to think about it while I was in the process of writing this book. Then one day, while I was out and he was away, he texted me: *Mom, right now I am really wanting your pancetta pasta. In fact, put that down as my favorite in your book!* I was happy and surprised to read his words. I had not made my pancetta pasta dish for a while, but it is a recipe that I put together by accident many years ago while on vacation.

1 pound spaghetti
3 tablespoons olive oil
1 shallot, chopped
1/2 pound pancetta, diced
2 tablespoons tomato paste
1 cup chicken stock
Freshly ground black pepper
1/3 cup Parmigiano-Reggiano cheese, grated
Fresh parsley

In a large pot, boil water for the spaghetti. When water begins to boil, add salt liberally. Let water return to a boil, and cook spaghetti to al dente. Reserve a cup of the pasta water and set aside. In a large sauté pan, warm olive oil over medium heat. Add shallot and cook until tender. Add pancetta and cook until crisp. Stir in tomato paste and chicken stock. Season with pepper. Allow ingredients in sauté pan to cook over high heat for one minute. Lower heat, and gently simmer for five minutes. Drain the spaghetti and add to sauté pan, tossing all ingredients well. Add some of the reserved water, as needed. Plate in a family-style platter or in warmed individual bowls. Garnish with fresh parsley.

Nicholas: Roasted Peppers with Capers, Anchovies, and Olives

There are few things that can compare to the mystery and beauty of an individual with autism. My son Nicky is nonverbal. He and I have never had a conversation, nor do I actually know what his exact thoughts entail. Yet, the connection of love and emotions that bind my son and I together is starkly calming and beautiful. Even though he cannot tell me about his world, I certainly know his world, and I believe that I am accurate in what is important to him, what he loves, what he enjoys, and what he values.

On the lighter side of life as a mom of a child with autism, the love of food has always been something that Nicky and I share together. It is an unspoken foodship. If one were to ask me what my son loves to eat and what I believe he favors most among my cooking and recipes, I could begin a very informative list. But throughout Nicky's entire life, from early childhood, he has always loved foods that are bright red in color. I often thought that this might have something to do with his autism, which involves some sensory issues. He loves to eat sweet, rosy apples; bright, firm tomatoes; spaghetti with succulent red sauce; and his greatest and most favorite food is roasted red peppers.

This recipe was taught to me by my mother and aunts, and it is served at many fine Italian restaurants. I have such a distinct feeling of pleasure when Nicky enjoys fresh roasted red peppers. The flavor is outstanding, and they are healthy. In addition, this truly says to me that it really can be one happy and meaningful life as long as we learn to deal with what life chooses to hand us.

8 large red peppers

1/4 cup extra-virgin olive oil

2 garlic cloves, chopped

1 tablespoon chopped anchovy fillets, plus oil from the jar or can

2 tablespoons capers

2 tablespoons sliced black olives

Kosher salt, to taste

Remove core and seeds completely from the peppers. Rinse out the inside, and shake out any lingering seeds. Leaving peppers whole, place on a baking dish or pan and roast in a preheated oven at 400°F. Turn occasionally, until skin is blackened and blistered. Transfer peppers to a large bowl, sealing the bowl tightly with plastic wrap, for 30 minutes. The blackened skin will loosen from the pepper. Gently peel off the blackened skin. If bits of black remain, that is fine. Cut each pepper into strips. Gently toss the peppers with the olive oil, garlic, anchovy fillets, capers, olives, anchovy oil, and salt. Serve roasted peppers with aged chunks of Auricchio Provolone, cured olives, and crusty bread.

Frankie: Chicken Francese

On the first page of this book, I wrote about entering my kitchen after my son's passing in order to cook his favorite dish. I did not reveal exactly what that dish was. For the very last recipe of my cookbook, I now come full circle to share it with you: chicken francese. Since Frankie's passing, I have continued to serve this dish to family and friends, and especially new friends. It is remarkable to me how I can truly share my son through this dish to those who never knew him. The fact that food can accomplish such a thing just amazes me, and this is what foodships is all about.

As I write this final page, I can still hear Frankie telling me why he liked my chicken francese so very much: "It's all about that deep lemon buttery flavor, Mom." A picture of my chicken francese graces the cover of this book, and I hope you will enjoy this recipe as much as my son did. I also hope that I have inspired you to value the connection of food and relationships and to recognize and cherish the foodships in your own life.

Always remember that life is one long adventure where every avenue and road we take, we can always find time to gather together to love, live, share, and eat, one recipe at a time!

1 pound chicken cutlets, pounded thin

Kosher salt and freshly ground black pepper

1/2 cup Bisquick

3 large eggs

1/4 cup extra virgin olive oil

1 tablespoon, plus 2 tablespoons butter

2 tablespoons flour

1/2 cup dry white wine

1 cup chicken stock

Juice of one lemon

Flat-leaf parsley, chopped

Cut the chicken cutlets into medallion size pieces and lightly season with salt and pepper. In a shallow dish, whisk the Bisquick, salt and pepper. Beat the eggs in another dish. Dredge the chicken medallions through the Bisquick, and then dip them in the egg. Warm the olive oil and one tablespoon of the butter in a sauté pan over medium heat. Fry the chicken medallions in batches, two minutes on each side. Season lightly with salt when they come hot out of the pan, and keep warm on a platter under a loose piece of tinfoil.

Add the two additional tablespoons of butter, and the flour, to the drippings of the sauté pan and mix well for a few moments. Add the wine, stock, and lemon juice, and simmer. Season with more salt and pepper. Return the chicken to the pan and cook in the sauce for two to three minutes. Serve with lemon slices, and garnish with parsley.

Acknowledgements

I would like to thank everyone that supported me during the writing of this cookbook. Your enthusiasm and commitment throughout this endeavor will never be forgotten. That in itself is an extraordinary "Foodship!"

To my mother, Josephine Orrichio, who lovingly and patiently listened as I wrote and re-wrote the many pages. Thank you for your unsurpassed advice and reminders of points I would sometimes forget.

To my dad, Anthony L. Orrichio, who cooked and baked for years with a true passion. Thank you for always telling me, "You can do it." I wish you were here to see the final outcome.

To my sister, Lucy Bruno, and my brother, Anthony Orrichio, who extended their unconditional support every step of the way. Life would not be what it is without you.

To my niece and nephews, Christina Bruno, Anthony Bruno and Anthony Arthur Orrichio, you all played such a unique and active role in making this book happen. I love all three of you very much.

To Veronica Clevidence and Sean McNamara, your editorial expertise has proven to be invaluable; thank you for being such genuine individuals.

To Sandra Speer, thank you for our decades of one long and adventurous friendship and for your unique culinary input.

To Camille and Phil Mouquinho, thank you for being such an important part of celebrating this cookbook. I am so happy to call you my friends.

To Marianne Teta, who in the spirit of loving sisterhood helped me decide on the right title. Our many 6:00 a.m. text messages really paid off!

To Vicki Wellington, Diane Anderson, John Knuckle and Sean Fedora, thank you for responding with such kindness. You made this process a better one.

To Anthony Giliberti, for your culinary critique, brotherly help and for always reminding me that food is happiness.

To Kayla Hernandez and Allison Carbonaro, who tirelessly and lovingly worked by my side during the testing of countless recipes.

To Sylvester Sichenze, for your true friendship and honest council whenever I reached out.

To Billy Park, my gratitude for helping me in the final stages of this project and for your generosity of spirit that stretched all the way from California to New York.

I would also like to thank all those who made such important contributions to this book: Jenelle Alza, Angie Biscuiti, Kevin Breen, Alice Campbell, Dave Campbell, Father John Bashobora,

Jenny Cheong, Susan Valdes-Dapena, The Ewen Family, Adrian Herzfeld, Bob Kazakov, Frank Kazeroid, The Lane Family, The Lynch Family, Chef Enzo Niglio, Susan Niglio, Chef Pnina Peled, John Trimboli and Janet Villamagna.

Finally, to my three sons, Frankie, who completely believed in me and watches over us from above, Nicky, who inspires me every moment, and Chris, who amazes me with every step he takes forward in life. This book is for all three of you, written with love.
⌇ C.L.

www.CamillesCooking.com

Made in the USA
Charleston, SC
15 January 2014